The Moving Body

The Moving Body

Teaching creative theatre

JACQUES LECOQ

in collaboration with
JEAN-GABRIEL CARASSO and JEAN-CLAUDE LALLIAS

Translated from *Le Corps poétique* by
DAVID BRADBY

Methuen Drama

Methuen Drama

Methuen Drama, an imprint of Bloomsbury Publishing Plc.

3 5 7 9 10 8 6 4

First published in Great Britain in 2000 by Methuen Publishing Limited
This revised edition published by Methuen in 2002
Reissued with a new cover design by Methuen Drama in 2009

Methuen Drama
Bloomsbury Publishing Plc
50 Bedford Square
WC1B 3DP
www.methuendrama.com

First published in French by Actes Sud-Papiers copyright © 1997

Copyright © The Estate of Jacques Lecoq, Jean-Gabriel Carasso,
Jean-Claude Lallias 1997

Translation copyright © David Bradby 2000

Photographs © Michèle Laurent, Alain Chambaretaud,
Patrick Lecoq, Richard Lecoq, Dodi Disanto 1997

David Bradby has asserted his rights under the
Copyright, Designs and Patents Act, 1988, to be identified
as the translator of this work

A CIP catalogue record for this book
is available from the British Library

ISBN 978 1 408 11146 8

Available in the USA from Bloomsbury Academic & Professional,
175 Fifth Avenue/3rd Floor, New York, NY 10010.
www.BloomsburyAcademicUSA.com

Typeset by Deltatype Ltd, Birkenhead, Merseyside
Printed and bound in Great Britain

CONTENTS

Contents

FOREWORD

Jacques Lecoq was a man of vision. He had the ability to see well. This vision was both practical and radical. As a young physiotherapist after the Second World War, he saw how a man with paralysis could organise his body in such a way that he could re-learn to walk, and taught him to do so. To actors he showed how the great movements of nature correspond to the most intimate movements of human emotion.

Like a gardener, he read not only the seasonal changes of his pupils but constantly seeded new ideas. During the 1968 student uprisings in Paris, when the pupils proposed the idea that they might teach themselves, he introduced the practice of *auto-cours*. This was a period of time in which groups of pupils collectively explored their own response to the week's work by devising a short piece of theatre to be presented before Jacques and the class. The growth of this idea took such a strong root that it remained central to his conception of the imaginative development and individual responsibility of the theatre artist. Like an architect, his analysis as to how the human body functions in space was linked directly to how we might unravel the structure of drama itself. Like a poet, he made us listen to individual words, before we even formed them into sentences, let alone plays.

What he offered in his school was, in a word, preparation – of the body, of the voice, of the art of collaboration (of which theatre is the most extreme artistic representation) and of the imagination. He was interested in creating a site to build on, not a finished edifice.

Contrary to what people often think, he had no style to propose. He offered no solutions. He only posed questions. When I last saw him, six months before he died, in his house under the shadow of Mont Blanc, to talk about a book we wished to make, he said with typical modesty: 'I am nobody. I am a neutral point through which you must pass in order to better articulate your own theatrical voice. I am only there to place obstacles in your path, so that you can better find your way around them.' As a result, we were constantly engaged in finding other ways of seeing. Constantly challenged to look again. Constantly alert to what is unexpected in the chaotic ever-changing patterns in nature and in our own natures.

'*Tout bouge*' [Everything moves] was the title of his lecture demonstration, but was also a central tenet of his teaching. And so when I pick up this book, I am at once delighted to be reminded of the tone of Jacques' voice and also acutely aware of him observing me. Suggesting at once that an idea, a phrase, an observation that is made here has less to do with, God forbid, an instruction manual, but is more a perspective on his constantly shifting teaching, caught in words, at one specific moment in time.

Jacques was a man of extraordinary perspectives. But for him perspective had nothing to do with distance. For him there were no vanishing points, only clarity, diversity and – supremely – coexistence. I can't thank you, but I see you surviving time, Jacques, longer than the ideas that others have about you.

Simon McBurney, 2000

BIOGRAPHICAL NOTE

Jacques Lecoq was an exemplary teacher. Over a period of more than forty years, his pedagogic practice was the seedbed in which his pupils could grow, each in his own way. Lecoq respected differences of culture, talent, physique: all who came to him were encouraged to develop according to their own peculiar gifts. For a long time he was a prophet without honour in his own country. While many of the most creative actors in contemporary theatre, as well as writers, directors, designers, architects, psychologists and teachers, based their artistic practice on his pedagogy, its principles were little known or understood by those who had not participated in the life of the school. No doubt this was partly because his teaching was so profoundly rooted in the body. It taught the essential laws of physical movement in space.

He was born on 15 December 1921 in Paris. As a young man, he was attracted by sports of all kinds. He joined a gymnastics club at the age of seventeen and then studied at a college of physical education. During the German occupation of France he joined with a group of young enthusiasts who sought to use gymnastics, mime, movement and dance to express opposition to the prevailing Fascist ideology. This led him on, after the liberation of France, to develop experimental performance work in which movement and theatre combined. In the first section of *The Moving Body*, entitled 'Personal Journey', he describes the countries he visited, the artists he met and the theatres he worked in during his formative period in the ten years following the end of the Second World War.

In 1956 he founded his own school in Paris, and the rest of the book describes the development of the school, setting out the methods of teaching which he developed there. Word gradually spread about this unorthodox training, whose method was to apply the laws of movement to dramatic creation and to different acting traditions, including masked performance, tragedy, melodrama, *commedia dell'arte*, clowning and *bouffons*. All of these terms took on special meanings through his teaching, and have acquired fresh life through the work of his pupils all over the world. He continued to take classes right up until the day before his death, on 19 January 1999. The École Internationale de Théâtre Jacques Lecoq continues his teaching, under the direction of his wife Fay Lecoq, at 57 rue du Faubourg-Saint-Denis, 75010 Paris, France.

BIBLIOGRAPHY AND FILMOGRAPHY

In addition to publishing numerous articles and interviews, Jacques Lecoq edited one other book: *Le théâtre du geste* (Paris: Bordas, 1987). A collection of articles in English about his work, edited by Franc Chamberlain and Ralph Yarrow, under the title *Jacques Lecoq and the British Theatre*, was published by Routledge in 2001.

In 1998/9 two 45-minute films were made with Jacques Lecoq by Jean-Noël Roy, Jean-Gabriel Carasso and Jean-Claude Lallias, entitled *Les deux voyages de Jacques Lecoq*. As well as passages in which Lecoq talks of his work and inspiration, these films include scenes in which his students can be seen working on several of the exercises he describes in *The Moving Body*. There are also interviews with actors and directors such as Dario Fo, Ariane Mnouchkine, Luc Bondy, Simon McBurney and many others. The film was a combined production by La Sept ARTE, On Line Productions and ANRAT and was first broadcast by ARTE in spring 1999. An English-language subtitled version may be had on video-cassette by applying to ANRAT, 13 bis rue Henry Monnier, 75009 Paris, France. Tel: 01 45 26 22 22; Fax: 01 45 26 16 20; e-mail: anrat@wanadoo.fr

In the 1960s, Lecoq made 26 short comic films under the title *La belle équipe* for the ORTF. These are now lodged at INA (Institut National de l'Audiovisuel, 83 rue Patay, 75013 Paris, France. Tel: 01 44 23 12 12), where they may be viewed by appointment. A selection of them is also held at the Maison Jean Vilar, 8 rue Mons, 84000 Avignon, France. Tel: 04 90 86 59 64.

The school also possesses in its archives a large number of videotapes recording the vast majority of Jacques Lecoq's courses spread over the two seasons of the teaching cycle.

TRANSLATOR'S NOTE

The original French text of Jacques Lecoq, Jean-Claude Lallias and Jean-Gabriel Carasso is characterised by clarity, lightness and an absence of complicated phraseology; I have tried to match these enviable qualities in my English translation. I have avoided technical terms when everyday words will serve as well, but, in a few cases, the special meaning attached to a French term requires that it be translated by an unusual English word. This is especially true where the French term is itself a neologism. The few examples of this kind can be listed here:

(1) *mimage* (a neologism) is translated by the same word, containing as it does both 'mime' and 'image'.

(2) *bouffon* is also translated by the same word, since the English 'buffoon' is too limited in scope. The French word suggests a grotesque comic while retaining overtones of medieval mummers and licensed court fools such as the one who accompanies King Lear in Shakespeare's tragedy.

(3) *Jouer* and *le jeu* are key words for Lecoq. They can be translated by many different words in English: to play/play; to act/acting; to perform/performance are all appropriate in various cases, but the noun 'play' can be confusing since in English it also designates a written drama. As the notion of playing is so central to improvisation, and since improvisation has a central role in Lecoq's teaching method, I have translated *jeu* and *rejeu* by 'play' and 'replay' wherever possible, sometimes substituting 'acting' or 'performing' for 'play' where the sense requires it.

I have used the masculine pronoun to apply to both males and females; similarly, words such as 'actor', which are not gender-specific, refer to men or women.

There is a full glossary of key words and phrases at the back of this book (see page 174).

To my wife, Fay Lecoq

I

PERSONAL
JOURNEY

1

From Sport to Theatre

I came to theatre by way of sports. At seventeen I discovered the geometry of movement through exercising on the parallel and horizontal bars at a Paris gymnastics club known as En Avant. The movement of the body through space demanded by gymnastic exercise is of a purely abstract order. In doing these physical movements I discovered extraordinary sensations which could be carried over into everyday life. On my way home in the metro, I would go over them in my mind. I would then sense all the rhythms perfectly, far more than in reality. I used to train at the Roland-Garros Stadium. I would run up for the high jump, then spring with the sensation of clearing a two-metre bar. I adored running, but it was the pure poetry of athletics which attracted me most: the contraction or elongation of the runners' shadows thrown by the sun slanting across the stadium when the rhythm of running sets in. This physical poetry had a powerful effect on me.

In 1941 I attended a college of physical education,[1] where I met Jean-Marie Conty. He had been top of his year at the École Polytechnique, was an international basketball player, had piloted planes for the Aéropostal company with Saint-Exupéry,[2] and was in charge of physical education for all of France. His friendship with Antonin Artaud[3] and Jean-Louis Barrault[4] led him to take an interest in the links between sport and theatre. It was thanks to him that, during the German Occupation, I discovered the theatre through Barrault's demonstration of the man–horse.[5] This discovery aroused a strong emotional response in me. Jean-Marie Conty helped to set up L'Education par le jeu dramatique (EPJD) [Education Through Dramatic Performance], a school based on unconventional methods founded by Jean-Louis Barrault with Roger Blin, André Clavé, Marie-Hélène Dasté and Claude Martin.[6] Later, in 1947, I was to teach physical expression at this school.

My first theatre training was with Travail et Culture (TEC) [Work and Culture].[7] With Claude Martin, who had been a pupil of Charles Dullin,[8] we would practise 'mimed improvisations', and with Jean Séry, a former dancer with the ballet company of the Paris Opera but now a convert to modern dance, we would improvise choreography to *The Hymn to the Sun* or *The Fire Dance*. As we were athletes (one of my companions, Gabriel Cousin, was a fine runner as well as a poet and playwright) our fundamental gestural language was based on the sports we practised: I was a swimmer, he was a runner. Sports, movement and theatre were already closely related.

After the Liberation of France in 1944, following on from my experiences with TEC, a group of us set up a troupe known as *Les Aurochs*. Then we linked up with Luigi Ciccione (our physical education teacher from the Bagatelle college), Gabriel Cousin and Jean Séry and founded Les Compagnons de la Saint-Jean. Throughout this heady period of post-war freedom, we put on large-scale festive events such as the first pilgrimage of the French Scouts to Puy-en-Velay, under the direction of Georges Douking, and the homecoming of the prisoners of war to Chartres. The arrival of a train carrying prisoners was re-enacted: we sang, we danced, and we mimed to the songs of Charles Trenet on the walls of the town, watched by thousands of people gathered on the grass. When we performed at Grenoble, Jean Dasté came to see us, and invited several of us to join the company he was putting together called Les Comédiens de Grenoble.[9] That was my professional début in theatre. I took on responsibility for physical training within the company. It was not a question of training athletes, but of training dramatic characters such as a king, a queen – a natural extension of the gestures acquired through sports. I hardly noticed the difference.

Through Jean Dasté I discovered masked performance and Japanese Noh theatre, both of which have had a powerful influence on me. In *L'Exode* [*Exodus*], a performance using mask and mime created by Marie-Hélène and Jean Dasté, every actor wore a 'noble' mask, which we nowadays call the neutral mask. I also have a vivid memory of a Japanese Noh play, *Sumidagawa* [*Sumida River*], in which we mimed the movements of a boat while our voices evoked the sounds of the river. We drew our inspiration from Jacques Copeau, who had been Dasté's teacher, as we performed in Grenoble and the surrounding region. I discovered the spirit of 'Les Copiaux',[10] their ambition to take theatre that spoke simply and directly to unsophisticated audiences. Copeau became a reference point for my work, alongside Dullin who belonged to the same theatrical family. Our youthful enthusiasm found its echo in the school Dullin had founded in Paris.

I left Grenoble at the end of 1947 to teach at the EPJD, then I moved to Koblenz, Germany, where I worked as an *animateur dramatique*[11] as part of a programme bringing together young people from France and Germany. For six months, working in teacher-training colleges in the Rhineland, I gave my first lecture-demonstrations, using the 'noble' mask to guide both teachers and students towards a discovery of movement and dramatic expressivity. I like to think I helped a little in the 'denazification' of Germany: I tried out a relaxation exercise which consisted of lifting the arm and letting it drop. I found that their way of doing the gesture was stiffer and different from ours, so I taught them to loosen up!

Italian adventure

In 1948, at the request of Gianfranco de Bosio and Lieta Papafava (two students who had come to Paris to do the course at the EPJD), I went to work in Italy for three months. I stayed for eight years. I had the good fortune to start at the University of Padua, where I was able to work both as teacher and creative practitioner. Here I discovered the *commedia dell'arte*. Since we needed masks, de Bosio introduced me to the sculptor Amleto Sartori, who placed his studio at our disposal. I myself fashioned the first masks out of cardboard, using Dasté's method, until, one day, Sartori offered to turn his own hand to the task. What a stroke of luck! He became the first person to rediscover the original techniques, which had almost died out, for making the leather masks of the *commedia*. In Padua I would go to the livestock market to watch the peasants selling their cattle, then Sartori would take me to a bar out of town, where we ate smoked horsemeat surrounded, as he would say, by 'horse thieves'. In these outlying districts I got the feel of the authentic *commedia dell'arte*: dramas in which the characters are permanently seized by an urgent passion for life. It was not a bookish *commedia*, but the *commedia* of Ruzzante,[12] rooted in peasant life, closely connected to its Italian origins.

At that time we contributed to restoring Ruzzante's reputation by performing one of his neglected plays: *La moschetta* [*The Coquette*]. Carlo Ludovici, the Harlequin in Cesco Baseggio's famous Venetian dialect company, taught me the different characters' body positions and attitudes which he himself had learned from an ageing Harlequin. Starting from these gestures and movements, I perfected a 'gymnastics of Harlequin' which I was then able to hand on to others in my turn. These discoveries were of major importance for the development of my work.

At the invitation of Giorgio Strehler and Paolo Grassi,[13] I then went to the Piccolo Teatro in Milan, where we set up the Piccolo drama school. You cannot open a school inside a company without automatically confronting a basic question: how do you ensure that its teaching is not limited just to the work of that company but extends to all other styles of theatre? A company-based school is inevitably ambiguous, because the director is bound to want to shape students in his own image and then to persuade the best of them to join his company. I am not in favour of this practice, which tends to limit work to a uniform style. Luckily, the Piccolo had no small roles to offer its students, as they had their own, extremely good actors. During this period I introduced Sartori to Strehler and he began making masks for the Piccolo.

When I was asked to be movement director for the chorus

in Sophocles' *Electra*, I had no idea that I was about to make another major discovery at the Piccolo: that of Greek tragedy and its chorus. I pursued my research into Greek choruses at Syracuse in Sicily, as movement director for productions of *Ion*, *Hecuba*, *Seven Against Thebes* and *Herakles*. At that time the convention was for the chorus passages to be danced in expressionist style. I was obliged to invent new gestures if I was to renew chorus movements whose form had atrophied over time. I could not then imagine how much this work would later come to influence my own teaching methods.

My Italian sojourn included various other adventures. Franco Parenti, an actor at the Piccolo, invited Dario Fo (who had just left the Milan Fine Arts College), Giustino Durano, an actor and singer, Fiorenzo Carpi, the music director of the Piccolo, and myself to put on a political review about contemporary life in Italy. It was called *Il dito nell'occhio* [*A Poke in the Eye*] and was followed, a year later, by *I sani da legare* [*Lunatic Sanity*]. These shows revived the radical spirit of Italian satire, both through their political commitment and through the physical language we used. They were also extremely successful at the box office. Together with Parenti, I went on to found the Parenti-Lecoq company, whose aim was to put on the work of new writers. It proved difficult since all the money we had earned on the satirical revues was lost putting on *Les Chaises* [*The Chairs*] and *La Cantatrice chauve* [*The Bald Prima Donna*] by Ionesco in 1951–52 and *Il diluvio* [*The Flood*] by Ugo Betti.

In the same period I put on *Mime Music No. 2* by Luciano Berio and was his first choreographer. Then Anna Magnani[14] signed me up as movement director for *Qui est en scène?* [*Who's on Stage?*], a revue which marked her return to the theatre after a long career in films. Helping this great lady of theatre to get back in touch with her audience was an unforgettable experience. Finally I took part, as an actor, in the first variety show for Italian television, presenting a number of comic pantomimes. Besides this, I did a bit of cinema acting, Hollywood-style. I have memories of morning jogs through Cinecittà studios, passing one film set after the other.

Back to Paris

I returned to Paris in 1956 with the two fundamental discoveries I had made in Italy: Italian *commedia dell'arte*, and Ancient Greek tragedy and its chorus. As a leaving present, Amleto Sartori gave me a set of leather *commedia* masks, allowing me to make them known in France and beyond. I very soon opened my school with a small group of students and at the same time was creating new work.

My first French experiment was to introduce masked acting in *La Famille Arlequin* [*The Harlequin Family*], a show put on by Jacques Fabbri and Claude Santelli with a team including several young, little-known actors: Raymond Devos, Rosy Varte, Claude Piéplu, André Gilles, Charles Charras. Philippe Tiry also took part in the venture. After that came the Théâtre National Populaire, where I worked for three years as movement director for Jean Vilar's productions.[15] When he hired me, Vilar said: 'The one thing I don't want is mime!' He soon realised that when I spoke of 'mime' it was something quite different from conventional mime as practised at that time. In addition, I directed Gabriel Cousin's[16] play *L'Aboyeuse et l'automate* [*The Barking Woman and the Automaton*] at the Théâtre Quotidien de Marseille. At this time I also worked for Marcel Bluwal on French television youth programmes. I wrote and directed twenty-six silent comic films in a series entitled *La Belle Equipe* [*The Great Team*], produced by Ange Casta and with actors from the school.

The school developed rapidly and I had to make a choice. I took the decision to devote myself completely to teaching, with the aim not just of starting an acting studio but of founding a whole school of theatre. I have always loved teaching, seeing it as a path to my own greater knowledge and understanding of movement. Through teaching I have discovered that the body knows things about which the mind is ignorant. This research into body and movement has been my passion and I still long to share it with others.

A school in motion

The school opened on 5 December 1956 at 94 rue d'Amsterdam, close to the Place de Clichy in Paris, then moved, one month later, into the dance studios at 83 rue du Bac, in the seventh arrondissement, where it stayed for eleven years. Teaching began with the neutral mask and physical expression, *commedia dell'arte*, Greek tragedy and chorus, white pantomime, figurative mime, expressive masks, music, and a technical grounding in dramatic acrobatics and mimed actions. Very soon I added work on spoken improvisation and on writing. We worked from silence towards the spoken word by means of what was to become the main training feature of the school: The Journey.

Three years later, in 1959, I started a company with a few of the students: Lilianne de Kermadec, Hélène Chatelain, Nicole de Surmont, Philippe Avron, Claude Evrard, Isaac Alvarez, Yves Kerboul, Elie Pressman, Edouardo Manet. With them, I developed a production entitled *Carnets de voyage* [*Travel Journals*]. Its aim was to show the different possibilities of mime as I understood it, relating it to both theatre and dance. The production included a masked chorus with *musique concrète*, figurative mime, white pantomime, a comic turn, melodrama and *commedia dell'arte*.

In 1962, for the first time, the clowns made their appearance as part of the training process. By exploring the domain of the ridiculous and the comic, I discovered the search for the clown within oneself, which was to liberate the actor from himself. This exploration opened up a vast dramatic territory which found its place in a number of further productions. In the same period I began to work with the Basel carnival masks (featureless larval masks), before they had been painted for the festival, and I also began to explore scripted plays.

In 1968 the school had outgrown the dance studios and we migrated to an industrial building in the rue de la Quintinie, once

The main studio at the school in the rue du Faubourg-Saint-Denis, Paris

used to manufacture aeronautical balloons. In this new space, the school took on its present form. We began to work on companies of clowns. For the first time, we gave commissions to the first-year students: this meant sending them off to investigate their chosen themes in different environments in order to provide material for the performances which they would then put on at the school's open evenings. The revolutionary events of May 1968 strengthened the teaching of the school and the desire of students to work there. We were, I suppose, one of the few schools to stay open in Paris during that period of unrest. While the student movement exploded onto the streets, we were exploding the traditions of gesture and text in search of a new language and new meanings. The same year I was invited by Jacques Bosson, a particularly imaginative architect and teacher, to join the École Nationale Supérieure des Beaux-Arts.[17] I began my research into built environments and adapted my movement teaching for the training of architects. These experiments were to last twenty years and contributed a great deal to my theatre knowledge, especially in the exploration of performance space. Out of this work developed a department of scenography within the school known as L.E.M. (Laboratoire d'Etude du Mouvement) [Laboratory for the Study of Movement].

Finding a place

From 1972 to 1976 the school was bundled from one place to another, from the Théâtre de la Ville to the American Centre on the boulevard de Raspail (a vast, unheated space in which we worked on lessons wrapped in blankets), with a brief return to the rue de la Quintinie. In these very difficult conditions, I discovered more dramatic territories, which were to enlarge the scope of my teaching and lead down many new paths: melodrama and *bouffons*, cartoon mime, storytelling mime. Pictorial pantomime replaced verbal pantomime. Melodrama struggled against over-blown cliché acting, to reveal strong, hidden emotions. The *bouffons* made use of every kind of raucous parody, giving birth to

11

a new, sacred dimension. Storytellers discovered new gestural languages. In 1976 we finally arrived at the space that seemed destined for us: 57 rue du Faubourg-Saint-Denis. It was Le Central, previously a well-known boxing centre, built a hundred years before in 1876, where the gymnastic methods of Amoros (the pioneer of physical education in France) had been practised. How symbolic! Here the crowds and the orators, who had emerged from the protest movement of 1968, took on new life. Out of this experience we rediscovered the humanity of the tragic chorus, just as melodrama showed us the humanity of the hero, replacing him in everyday situations. The *commedia dell'arte*, which had grown inflexible, did a back flip and turned itself inside out. It succeeded in liberating that 'human comedy' from which it had been born but which it had gradually forgotten. The clowns lost their red noses in our productions, though they kept them in the classes. Comedy embraced the burlesque and the absurd with the renaissance of cabaret and variety shows. The *bouffons* opened up other terrains: the mysterious, the fantastic and the grotesque. Next came the time for blending all this through the chemistry of great drama: melodrama and the chorus (melo-chorus), clowns and grotesques, cartoon mime and drama, *bouffons* and mystery, melomime and so on.

Our primary pedagogic journey across the broad, horizontal landscape of dramatic styles (which I call territories) gradually opened the way to a second journey up and down vertical axes, both scaling the heights of different acting levels and exploring the depths of poetry. The dynamics of words, of colours, of passions, and the attempt to discover abstract, essential principles underlying all lived experience, led to the quest for a common denominator. But this quest implies the need for maintaining distance and, if possible, a sense of humour: one must never forget that the purpose of the journey is the journey itself.

Today the school is still in a state of constant movement and continues to develop. Every day the classes are different, but they follow a precise order of progression. The students may lead us to question certain aspects of our approach, but there is a continuity and the teaching method is highly structured. I am sometimes told: 'Because it is so structured, we have no freedom.' The opposite is true, however. Even though it sometimes looks, from the outside, as if we keep on doing the same thing, in reality everything changes – but slowly. We do not turn great somersaults, we are like the sea: the movement of the waves above is more visible than the currents beneath, but despite that there is movement in the depths. Even if, from time to time, we lift our heads above the water, we quickly return to the strong, steady flow of the underlying current. In December 1996 the school celebrated its fortieth birthday.

2

The Educational Journey

The education offered by the Lecoq school is spread over two years, during which students move along two parallel paths: on the one hand the study of improvisation and its rules and on the other movement technique and its analysis. These dual journeys are supplemented by *auto-cours* through which the students' own theatre work takes shape in small productions.

At the start we investigate psychological play, which is silent. Then, starting from a neutral state, a state combining calm and curiosity, the real educational journey begins with research into the dynamics of nature. Natural elements, materials, animals, colours, lights, sounds and words are discovered through the miming body and later enrich character acting. Different levels of acting are developed, from replay with expressive and character masks to abstract masks, forms and structures. The constraints of style create a different kind of reality. The technical part, based on movement analysis, follows a thematic series of improvisations. Exercises develop the receptive and expressive potential of the human body (physical and vocal preparation, dramatic acrobatics, analysis of physical actions). This first part of the journey includes approaches to the arts of poetry, painting and music.

The second part of the journey begins with a study of the language of gestures. This prepares students for an exploration of the full range of dramatic territories, their relations to one another, their share in the universal poetic awareness and for the setting up of different levels of acting. This geodramatic journey, as I call it, covers the ground in a three-dimensional way. It is based on five principal territories which generate others, all of which have commonly accepted names in the history of theatre:

1 Melodrama (grand emotions)
2 *Commedia dell'arte* (human comedy)
3 *Bouffons* (from grotesque to mystery)
4 Tragedy (chorus and hero)
5 Clowns (burlesque and absurd)

and to these should be added the varieties of Comedy.

Applied technique [i.e. technique applied to these different territories] lends a framework to acting, and the addition of dramatic texts enriches creativity in each area.

Different ways of using exercises are employed at each stage:

- the developmental method, from the simplest to the most complex
- the transfer method, from physical technique to dramatic expression (dramatic justification for physical actions, transfer of natural dynamics to characters and situations)
- expansion and reduction of gestures, from equilibrium to respiration
- scales and levels of acting
- linking of gesture and voice
- economy of movements, accidents and detours
- passage from the real to the imaginary
- the discovery of play and its rules (the rules arising out of play itself)
- the method of constraints (spatial, temporal and numerical)

The investigation of chosen themes presented through performance, and a technical examination (the linking of twenty movements) mark the end of the first year. At the conclusion of the second year the students receive their commissions to work on their own.

Presentations, linked to the themes explored in the course, are shown during the second year. These are all the students' own work, grouped together in an evening's public performance, and take place three times in each season.

Movement, as manifested in the human body, is our permanent guide in this journey from life to theatre.

A dynamic theatre of new work

The aim of the school is to produce a young theatre of new work, generating performance languages which emphasise the physical playing of the actor. Creative work is constantly stimulated, largely through improvisation, which is also the first approach to playwriting. The school's sights are set on art theatre, but theatre education is broader than the theatre itself. In fact my work has always nurtured a dual aim: one part of my interest is focused on theatre, the other on life. I have always tried to educate people to be at ease in both. My hope, perhaps utopian, is for my students to be consummate livers of life and complete artists on stage. Moreover, it is not just a matter of training actors, but of educating theatre artists of all kinds: authors, directors, scenographers as well as actors.

One of the school's unique features is to provide as broad and as durable a foundation as possible, since we know that each student will go on to make his own journey using the foundations we provide. Students we train acquire an understanding of acting and develop their imaginations. This allows them either to invent their own theatre or to interpret written texts, if they so desire, but in new ways. Interpretation is the extension of an act of creation.

Improvisation is at the heart of the educational process and is sometimes confused with expression. Yet a person expressing himself is not necessarily being creative. The ideal, of course, would be for creation and expression to go hand in hand, in perfect harmony. Unfortunately many people enjoy expressing themselves, 'letting it all hang out', and forgetting that they must not be the only ones to get pleasure from it: spectators must receive pleasure, too. There are many teachers who confuse these two points of view.

The difference between the act of expression and the act of

creation is this: in the act of expression one plays for oneself alone rather than for any spectators. I always look for an actor who 'shines', who develops a space around himself in which the spectators are also present. Many absorb this space into themselves, excluding spectators, and the experience becomes too private. If students feel better after doing the course, that is a bonus, but my aim is not to provide therapy through theatre. In any process of creation the object made no longer belongs to the creator. The aim of this act of creation is to bear fruit which then separates from the tree.

In my method of teaching I have always given priority to the external world over inner experience. In our work the search for self-enlightenment and for spiritual bliss has little attraction. The ego is superfluous. It is more important to observe how beings and objects move, and how they find a reflection in us. We must give priority to the horizontal and the vertical, to whatever exists outside ourselves, however intangible. People discover themselves in relation to their grasp of the external world, and if the student has special qualities, these will show up in the reflection. I do not search for deep sources of creativity in psychological memories whose 'cry of life mingles with the cry of illusion'. I prefer to see more distance between the actor's own ego and the character performed. This allows the performer to play even better. Actors usually perform badly in plays whose concerns are too close to their own. They adopt a sort of blank voice because they retain part of the text for themselves without being able to hand it on to the public. Neither belief nor identification is enough – one must be able genuinely to play.

My first response to any performer's improvisation or exercise is to make observations, which are not to be confused with opinions. When a car tyre bursts, that's not an opinion, it's a fact. I observe. Opinions can only be formulated afterwards, based on this observation of reality. Observations are made by the teacher surrounded by students. While I am observing, I sense the students anticipating what I shall say. My job is to articulate the

1st year

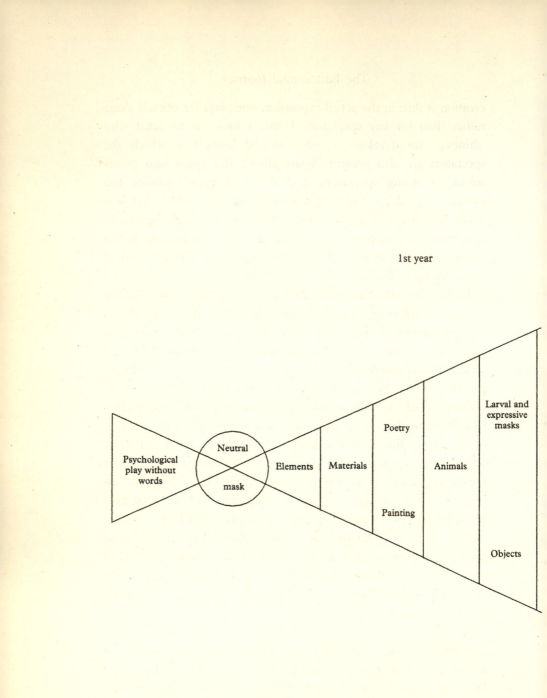

The Educational Journey of the
International School of Mime and Theatre

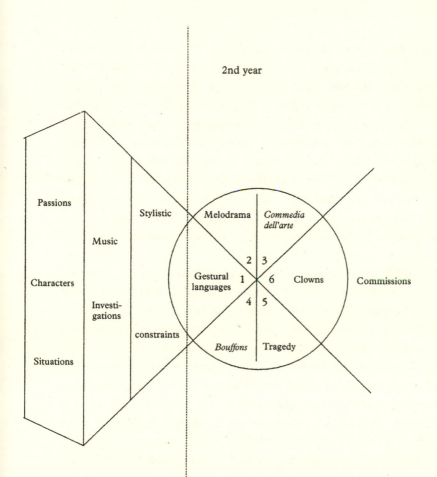

observation, but it must be shared by all. There is not much point, after seeing an improvisation, in a teacher saying 'that gave me pleasure', or 'I liked that a lot'. Different people will like different things. But for an observation to be made one must pay close attention to the living process, while trying to be as objective as possible.

The critical comments one makes about the work do not attempt to distinguish the good from the bad, but rather to separate what is accurate and true from what is too long or too brief, what is interesting from what is not. This might appear pretentious but the only thing which interests us is what is accurate and true: an artistic angle, an emotion, a colour combination. All these aesthetic elements can be found in any durable work of art, independent of its historical dimension. They can be sensed by anyone and an audience always knows perfectly well when something is accurate and true. They may not know why, but it is up to us to know, because we are, after all, specialists.

My comments are always related to the movement I see. Why did that bit of movement fade? Why did we feel that another bit would go on for ever? These are simple observations, placed at the service of a living structure. Now every living structure emerges from movement which rises and falls and has its own rhythm. This organic process can be found at work in every improvisation. In this sense, the school could also be seen as providing an education in seeing. Anyone can suggest a theme for an improvisation; it is far more difficult to comment on it afterwards. Rather than handing on a set body of knowledge, it is a question of reaching a common understanding. Master and student must both reach an enhanced level of insight. The master articulates for his students something which he would never have been able to formulate without them, permitting the students, through their commitment and curiosity, to assist at the birth of new insights.

Of course students also need to have their own point of view. In their work they must have ideas and opinions. But if these ideas are not grounded in reality, what use are they? The same phenomenon can be found in painting: Corot, Cézanne or Soutine were able to paint all kinds of trees, to transfigure them or to capture a particular facet, an unusual light for example, but if 'The Tree' had not been there in the painting, nothing would have happened. We always return to the observation of nature and to human realities. I have a strong belief in permanency, in the 'Tree of trees', the 'Mask of masks', the balance that sums up perfect harmony. I realise that this tendency of mine may become an obstacle, but it is one that is necessary. Starting from an accepted reference point, which is neutral, the students discover their own point of view. Of course there is no such thing as absolute and universal neutrality, it is merely a temptation. This is why error is interesting. There can be no absolute without error. I am fascinated by the difference between the geographic pole and the magnetic pole. The north pole does not quite coincide with true north. There is a small degree of difference, and it is lucky that this degree exists. Error is not just acceptable, it is necessary for the continuation of life, provided it is not too great. A large error is a catastrophe, a small error is essential for enhancing existence. Without error, there is no movement. Death follows.

The search for permanency

Alongside improvisation, the second major goal of the school concerns movement analysis. Movement is more than just a matter of covering the distance between points A and B. The important thing is *how* the distance is covered. The dynamics underlying my teaching are those of the relationship between rhythm, space and force. The laws of movement have to be understood on the basis of the human body in motion: balance, imbalance, opposition, alternation, compensation, action and reaction. These laws may all be discovered in the body of a spectator as well as in that of the actor. The spectator knows perfectly well when there is harmony or disharmony in a scene. The audience forms a collective body which recognises life, or the lack of it, in a performance. Collective boredom is a sign that the performance is not working organically.

The laws of movement govern all theatrical situations. A piece of writing is a structure in motion. Though themes may vary (they belong to the realm of ideas), the structures of acting remain linked to movement and to its immutable laws. If an architect designs a concrete arch with a span that is too wide, the whole thing collapses. In theatre you sometimes go too far without knowing whether there will be a collapse. We must be architects of the inner life. Outer movements resemble inner movements, they speak the same language. My main fascination is with the poetics of these permanencies, which give birth to writing.

I have always favoured a teaching method that uses open mime. To mime is a fundamental action, the foundation of dramatic creation, not only for the actor, but also for writing and for performance. For me, mime is central to theatre: being able to play at being someone else and to summon illusory presences constitutes the very body of theatre. Sadly, the word has become a trap, restricted and atrophied. So I have to clarify what I mean by mime. Mime became ossified as soon as it separated itself from theatre. It closed in upon itself and only an emphasis on virtuosity could give it any meaning. In the end, French theatre rejected it completely, expelled it and viewed it as a separate art form. But miming is a fundamental human action, a childhood action: children mime the world in order to get to know it and to prepare themselves to live in it. Theatre is a game which merely extends this action in different ways.[18]

To mime is literally to embody and therefore to understand better. A person who handles bricks all day long reaches a point where he no longer knows what he is handling. It has become an automatic part of his physical life. If he is asked to mime handling a brick, he rediscovers the meaning of the object, its weight and volume. This has interesting consequences for our teaching method: miming is a way of rediscovering a thing with renewed freshness. The action of miming becomes a form of knowledge.

This educational use of mime must not be confused with the art of mime, which reaches its highest expression in Japanese Noh theatre, when the actor mimes his anger by means of a few vibrations of his fan.

There is another form of hidden mime, which can be found in all the arts. Every true artist is a mime. Picasso's ability to draw a bull depended on his having found the *essential* Bull in himself, which released the shaping gesture of his hand. He was miming. Painters and sculptors are outstanding mime artists because they share in the same act of embodiment. There is a submerged form of mime which gives rise to different creative acts in all the arts. This is why I could move from teaching theatre to teaching architecture, and how I invented 'architect-mimes'. They mime existing spaces in order to know them better, then they mime what they will build, in order that their buildings will come to life.

For me mime is an integral part of theatre, not a separate art form. The mime which I love involves an identification with things in order to make them live, even when words are used. Italians understand this. I came to realise it when watching Marcello Moretti in *Harlequin, Servant of Two Masters*, or Vittorio Gassman or Dario Fo. This Italian-style comedy, using both gestures and words, was my inspiration, and I subsequently reinvented it through my teaching. That explains why I never put the word 'mime' on its own in the name of the school. I first used the wording 'Mime, Education of the Actor', then 'Mime and Theatre', 'Mime, Movement, Theatre', and finally 'International Theatre School' ['École Internationale de Théâtre'].

*

The great strength of the school lies in its students. They are constantly thrown back on themselves and have to invent their own theatre. We may suggest themes, offer advice or stimulate the students by imposing restraints, but we can never go any deeper until they are engaged by the work. Nevertheless, students are often contradictory. We must hear what they say without listening too much. We must also grapple with them if we are to lead them into a place of true poetry. This can be difficult to achieve. When they lack imagination we must goad them with fantastic visions of beauty, with the madness of beauty.

The teachers at the school have also shared in its development. All the teachers are former students, with the result that we share a common language and the same reference points, while each teacher brings his or her own personality to the mix. The search for scientific curiosity and for knowledge brings us together. Among the teachers who have contributed to the school, Antoine Vitez occupies a special place. He is the only one not to have been a student of mine. His first teaching assignment at the school was between 1967 and 1969. I had asked him to work on an approach to text, which we differentiate from textual interpretation. He was to retain this fundamental division in his later teaching at the Conservatoire National d'Art Dramatique.

Forty years after it first opened its doors, the school remains a place of ongoing research. With each day's work adding to our experience, our project becomes more interesting. Novelty is not, in itself, indispensable. Probing the depths of one strand leads to the discovery that everything is contained within it.

You can immerse your life in a drop of water and see the whole world!

II

THE WORLD AND ITS MOVEMENTS

Pulling and pushing exercises

A Blank Page

Students come from all over the world to our school and enrol in the first year for a trial term. Their average age is twenty-five, and they have some acting experience. Many who come from abroad have already completed drama school in their own country, others will have attended short courses and workshops. Because of this, we have to begin by stripping away learned behaviour patterns which do not belong to them, eliminating everything which might hinder them from rediscovering life at its most authentic. We have to divest the students of some of what they have learned, not in order to diminish their store of knowledge, but to create a blank page for them. In this way they can be awakened to that far-reaching curiosity that is essential if they are to discover the quality of play. This is the objective of the first year's work.

In the course of this first year of discovery and understanding we seed the roots of creative acting, by means of improvisation and the analysis of movement in life. A permanent link is established between these two activities. On the one hand, through improvisation, we externalise what is latent within the students; on the other, through objective study of movement techniques, we allow them to work from the outside in.

In the area of improvisation, there are successive stages which shape the first year's curriculum. Alongside these, movement analysis is also approached through a structured, developmental course. At the same time, students work on body and voice, and take classes in dramatic acrobatics, juggling and stage fighting.

Throughout the year we facilitate the students' own personal creative research by means of *auto-cours*: each week students are given a theme to work on without a teacher in whatever way they choose. This is their own theatre. It is essential to allow them this freedom, and it ensures that we never lose sight of the main goal of the school: creativity. It also allows them to apply everything that they have been learning in their classes, revealing the particular talents of each of the students, their feel for play and for dramatic writing.

The three main directions of the first year's work, set out separately in the following pages, are in reality overlapping and closely interwoven throughout the structure of the first year. Improvisation, movement analysis and personal creativity constantly connect and complement one another, bringing the students into the closest possible contact with the world and its movements.

1

Improvisation

Silence Before Words

Replay and play

We approach improvisation through psychological replay, which is silent. Replay involves reviving lived experience in the simplest possible way. Avoiding both transposition and exaggeration, remaining strictly faithful to reality and to the student's own psychology, with no thought for spectators, students bring a simple situation to life: a classroom, a market place, a hospital, the metro. Play [acting] comes later, at the point when, aware of the theatrical dimension, the actor can shape an improvisation for spectators, using rhythm, tempo, space, form. Play may be very close to replay or may distance itself through the most daring theatrical transposition, but it must never lose sight of the root anchoring it to reality. A large part of my teaching method involves making students understand this principle.

*

We begin with silence, for the spoken word often forgets the roots from which it grew, and it is a good thing for students to begin by placing themselves in the position of primal naivety, a state of innocent curiosity. In any human relationship two major zones of silence emerge: before and after speech. Before, when no words have been spoken, one is in a state of modesty which allows words to be born out of silence; in this state strength comes from avoiding explanatory discourse. By taking these silent situations, and working on human nature, we can rediscover those moments when the words do not yet exist. The other kind of silence comes

29

afterwards: when there is nothing more to be said. For us that one is not so interesting.

First improvisations allow me to observe the quality of each student's acting: How do they play very simple things? How do they keep silent? Some feel inhibited, forbidden to speak, whereas in fact I forbid nothing, I simply ask them to keep silent, the better to understand what lies beneath language.

There are only two ways out of this silence: speech or action. At a given moment, when silence becomes too highly charged, the theme breaks loose and speech takes over. So one may speak, but only where necessary. The other way is action: 'I'll do something.' At the start all the students are so keen to act that they throw themselves into situations irrespective of motivation. In so doing, they overlook the other players and fail to act with them. But true play can only be founded on one's reaction to another. They have to understand this essential fact: to react is to throw into relief suggestions that come from the external world. The interior world is revealed through a process of reaction to the provocations of the world outside. The actor cannot afford to rely on an interior search for sensitivities, memories, a childhood world.

Paradoxically, 'The Childhood Bedroom' is one of the oldest themes for improvisation, which I suggest at the beginning of the year.

> *You return after a long absence and revisit your childhood bedroom.*
> *You have had to travel a long way, you arrive at the door, you open it.*
> *How will you open it? How will you go in? You rediscover your*
> *bedroom: nothing has changed, each object is in its place. Once again*
> *you find all your childhood things, your toys, your furniture, your bed.*
> *These images of the past come alive again within you, until the*
> *moment when the present reasserts itself. And you leave the room.*

The theme is not the bedroom of my childhood, but a childhood bedroom, which you play at rediscovering. The dynamics of memory are more important than the memory itself. What happens when you find yourself confronted with a place that you think you are discovering for the first time? Suddenly, a memory is triggered: 'I've already seen that!' You are in an image of the present and suddenly an image of the past appears. Out of the interplay between these two images comes the improvisation. Naturally, anyone who improvises draws on his own memory, but that memory can also be imaginary.

I remember setting this improvisation during a short course in Germany. A girl had performed the rediscovery of a ring in her old jewellery box. Instinctively, she tried it on one finger, but it was too small, so she put it onto her little finger. Her improvisation had given rise to great emotion. Had she invented the ring? Was it a genuine memory? Improvisation sometimes stirs up things that are very intimate, but they belong to the person who performs them. I never ask students to search within themselves for the true memory. I have no wish to enter into their intimate secrets.

This exercise is played solo, in front of the other students. Since it is a performance given in front of spectators, I set no time limit, but am sensitive to the dramatic rhythm which is established, noting where it strikes true. The improvisation is mimed: in this way sensitivity to objects is renewed and many objects can be conjured up without the encumbrance of a single real object.

Waiting is the guiding 'theme' which informs the first silent improvisations. The chief motivating force lies in the look: to watch and be watched. Much of life is spent waiting; we wait with strangers at the post office, at the dentist. Waiting is never abstract. Different points of contact feed into it – actions and reactions. We seek to rediscover this through our improvisations, but also through observing real life. For acting requires more than memories drawn from life. We must constantly go back to live observation: watching people as they walk down the street, or waiting in a queue, attentive to the behaviour of others in the queue.

The theme I suggest is 'The Psychological Encounter', which I prefer to set in a clichéd context, very bourgeois, but which could also take place in any other space, even one that is undefined.

> *You have been invited, by a very rich lady, to take cocktails at around 5pm on a Friday. The guests have never met each other before. The floor is covered with a huge Persian carpet; a Venetian glass chandelier hangs from the ceiling; on one side of the room is a Renaissance painting, no doubt a forgery; on the other, a beautiful piece of Chinese porcelain stands on a little column. The apartment is on the second floor (the smartest floor to live on in Paris) doubtless in the seizième arrondissement, with a big 1920s bay window looking out over an avenue. At the back, a sideboard with cocktails, whisky, fruit juice, nibbles . . .*
>
> *Five characters present themselves, one after the other, at the entrance. A majordomo has let them in, they have come through a door, along a corridor and have been told: 'It's there!' The first to come in doesn't know that he will be the first, he arrives and there's no one else, just him. A second person arrives, then a third, a fourth, a fifth. The lady, of course, never appears! So they find themselves confronted with a silent situation, not daring to speak, rather as if they were in a waiting room.*

Work of this kind brings to light a number of possible detours or digressions. On the one hand there are the 'pantomimic' aspects, when the students replace the words they cannot say with gestures, or when they pull faces in order to express themselves. On the other hand, they often try to show that they have seen something before they have genuinely seen it. They are merely going through the motions. They perform the gesture before having found the sensation which motivates it. The first person to come in doesn't know he is the first. So this very important moment of surprise is established, and with it the timing that is essential to the art of acting. The actor knows the end of the play, but the character doesn't.

Another problem to emerge is the result of an actor copying the timescale and the physical distance established by the previous entries. The first two actors who enter establish a tempo, which must of necessity be disrupted by the third if the scene is to stay alive. They must find a rhythm rather than a tempo. Tempo is geometrical, rhythm is organic. Tempo can be defined, while rhythm is difficult to grasp. Rhythm is the result of an actor's response to another live performer. It may be found in waiting, but also in action. To enter into the rhythm is, precisely, to enter into the great driving force of life itself. Rhythm is at the root of everything, like a mystery. Of course I don't say that to the students, or they would no longer be able to do a thing. They must discover it for themselves.

Very often, in this type of situation, people take up symmetrical positions. They stand at an equal distance from one another, either in a line, side by side, one behind the other, or in a circle: it's similar to when they enter to the same tempo. Such positions can only serve military or ritual purposes; they are not dramatically playable. Every group will tend to arrange itself according to a geometrical pattern (not to be confused with dynamic geometry). Each character must be both part of the group and separate, must find his own rhythmic beat and his specific space.

The opposite situation also presents itself: someone enters and, desperate to seem original at all costs, behaves like a psychiatric case, adopting the most extravagant behaviour. This is at the opposite extreme from the fault of sheep-like mimicry. Of course it is not what we are looking for. But it may have an interestingly provocative effect on the others, giving them the opportunity to react, however awkward the situation may be. Their reaction is a group one: 'all against one'. A kind of chorus is born, out of the confrontation with this injured hero.

Towards the structures of play

After we have worked through this theme once, we return to a stripped-down version of the exercise. Ignoring its anecdotal interest, we turn the theme inside out in order to discover the motor which drives it. In this way other themes, images, situations, characters are introduced.

Two characters pass, each one meets the other's eye and comes to a stop, and a silent dramatic situation arises from this meeting. Then a third person comes along and observes the first two. Then a fourth who watches the first three, etc.

Little by little, the theme is rediscovered by accumulation, but only in its structure. There is no imagery or background given in advance, simply a dramatic motor which can be taken apart and analysed. From this basic structure, we can draw out and demonstrate a number of different sub-themes which can be grouped under the general theme of 'The Person Who . . .'. Reduced to this motor, psychological themes lose their anecdotal elements and reach a status of heightened play. They enable us to observe with great precision a particular detail which then becomes the major theme: 'The person who believes that . . . but he is wrong!' – the person who believes that someone is waiting for him, the person who believes he is hated, the person who believes he is the stronger, the person who believes he is being smiled at.

You are sitting in a café. Opposite you, at another table, someone makes a small hand gesture in your direction. You wonder if you know her or not. Out of politeness, you respond in the same way. The person opposite, put at ease, begins to gesture more wildly, making large movements, playing with an object, smiling. Little by little a complicity grows between you, a dialogue conducted in gestural signs or facial expressions. In the end the person gets up and comes towards you, smiling. You too get up, to greet her . . . but she passes beside you and goes on to someone behind you.

The important thing here is the rising dynamic scale [like a musical scale] which must be played for every nuance. Progressive playing of this situation leads to the building up of a genuine framework which, if taken further, resembles the performance structures of the *commedia dell'arte*. Situations are pushed to their limit: 'Someone is afraid, he draws back; Harlequin is afraid, he hides under the carpet or withdraws into himself!' We always try to push the situation beyond the limits of reality. We aim for a level of aesthetic reality which would not be recognisable in real life in order to demonstrate how theatre prolongs life by transposing it. This is a vital discovery for the students.

The notion of the scale clarifies the different phases in the progression of a dramatic situation. I have incorporated it in the theme of the 'Six Sounds' which we use as a technical improvisation in class.

You are in the middle of a manual task which involves the body in repetitive action (e.g. sawing wood, painting a wall, sweeping), and you will hear six sounds, each of which will have a different importance for you. The first one you do not hear (which does not mean there will be no reaction). The second, you hear, but without paying any special attention to it. The third one is loud and you listen to see if it will repeat. Since it does not, you cease paying attention. The fourth is very loud, and you think you know where it comes from, which reassures you. The fifth fails to confirm what you had thought. Finally the sixth and last is a jet plane which passes over your head.

This highly structured scale will become a reference point for all the other scales we shall meet subsequently, in a variety of dramatic situations. The exercise is especially useful for understanding the progressive dynamics of a movement, but also for the technical knowledge of the movements imposed by a scale. How is the action changed by the volume of the sounds? Are the gestures you make different according to the importance given to what you hear? What are the links between action and reaction?

In reply to these questions, we conclude that action must always precede reaction. The longer the interval between action and reaction, the greater will be the dramatic intensity and the more powerful will be the dramatic performance if the actor can sustain this level. Dramatic power will be commensurate with length of reaction time. The principle of the scale, which we use a great deal, is an excellent means for revealing this law and for demonstrating the levels of acting.

In the course of this work, I first point out the different articulations of the theme to the students, before they perform, then I beat out the sounds myself on a tambourine. I become the director of the exercise, which forces me to give a rhythm to the succession of different sounds. I cannot just beat them out at regular five-second intervals. I have to find the rhythm which is favourable to the performance: if I wait too long, or if I go too fast, the exercise is a failure. The teacher has to become a director for this class.

*

The aim of these initial exercises, taken as a whole, is to delay the use of the spoken word. The imposition of silent performance leads the students to discover this basic law of theatre: words are born from silence. At the same time they discover that movement, too, can only come out of immobility. 'Be quiet, play, and theatre will be born!', that could be our motto. It would provide a paradoxical counterpoint to the statues erected at the entrance to Khmer temples, one with an open mouth, the next closed. 'First you speak, then you keep silent,' they say. My teaching claims the exact opposite.

The Neutral Mask

Neutrality

Work with the neutral mask follows on from silent psychological play, but in fact it is the start of the journey. Experience has shown that such fundamental things occur with this mask that it has become the central point of my teaching method.

The neutral mask is an object with its own special characteristics. It is a face which we call neutral, a perfectly balanced mask which produces a physical sensation of calm. This object, when placed on the face, should enable one to experience the state of neutrality prior to action, a state of receptiveness to everything around us, with no inner conflict. This mask is a reference point, a basic mask,

36

The neutral mask created by Amleto Sartori for Jacques Lecoq

a fulcrum mask for all the other masks. Beneath every mask, expressive masks or *commedia dell'arte* masks, there is a neutral mask supporting all the others. When a student has experienced this neutral starting point his body will be freed, like a blank page on which drama can be inscribed.

*

A good neutral mask is very difficult to create. Naturally it has nothing in common with white masks used in carnival processions or demonstrations. Those are dead masks, at the opposite pole from neutrality. We use leather masks made by Amleto Sartori, which go back to the noble mask used by Dasté [see pages 5–6]. The noble mask had something Japanese about it, but the quality it shared with the neutral mask was its calm, lack of particular expression and state of equilibrium.

Like every other mask, a neutral mask should not adhere closely to the face. A certain distance should be preserved between the face and the mask, for it is precisely this distance which makes it possible for the actor to play. It must also be slightly larger than the face. The real dimensions of a face, as found, for example, on death masks, do not help the performer to find the register of play, nor to extend it to those around. This is true of all masks.

Essentially, the neutral mask opens up the actor to the space around him. It puts him in a state of discovery, of openness, of freedom to receive. It allows him to watch, to hear, to feel, to touch elementary things with the freshness of beginnings. You take on the neutral mask as you might take on a character, with the difference that here there is no character, only a neutral generic being. A character experiences conflict, has a history, a past, a context, passions. On the contrary, a neutral mask puts the actor in a state of perfect balance and economy of movement. Its moves have a truthfulness, its gestures and actions are economical. Movement work based on neutrality provides a series of fulcrum points that will be essential for acting, which comes later. Having experienced perfect balance, the actor is better equipped to express a character's imbalance or conflictual states. And for those who, in life, are always in conflict with themselves, with their own bodies, the neutral mask helps them to find a stable position where they can breathe freely. For everyone, the neutral mask becomes a point of reference.

Beneath the neutral mask the actor's face disappears and his body becomes far more noticeable. Talking to someone, you often look that person in the face. With an actor wearing the neutral mask, you look at the whole body. The look is the mask, so the face becomes the whole body. Every movement is revealed as powerfully expressive. When the actor takes off the mask, if he has worn it well, his face is relaxed. I hardly need to watch what he does; it is enough to observe his face at the end to know if he wore it truthfully. The mask will have drawn something from him, divesting him of artifice. His face will be beautiful, free. Once he has achieved this freedom, the mask can be removed with no fear of falling back on artificial gestures. The neutral mask, in the end, unmasks.

The first lesson is the discovery of the mask as object. I begin by showing the mask. The students handle it, wear it, try out different movements in order to experience it. These introductions are important, for the first contact with the mask sometimes provokes astonishing reactions: some people feel they are suffocating and cannot bear it on their face; others (rarer cases) tear it off. Each time students put on the mask for the first time, I ask them to express what they have felt, even if it's only a single word. Some say nothing, which is fine. Others 'discover their body' or observe that 'things go more slowly'. Such impressions, voiced immediately after the first experience of the mask, require no comment. They are truthful; I hear them out. It is not our job to say how one should act with the neutral mask. A technician might explain, but a teacher must hold back. Telling the students how to do it would be to hinder them from wearing the mask. They would be too worried about doing it right, whereas their primary need is to experience.

The first exercise we do when wearing the mask is 'Waking Up':

In a state of repose, relaxed, lying on the ground, I ask the students to 'wake up for the first time'. Once the mask is awake, what can it do? How can it move?

This theme is played out in front of other students in groups of seven or eight, but each one performs his own awakening. It is far from being a realistic improvisation: by specifying a first-time awakening, we are essentialising the theme, turning it into something generic.

This improvisation leads to regular observations. Some students have a tendency to first move their hands, then their feet, to discover their own bodies, while all along an extraordinary dimension is being offered to them: space. We have to explain that we aren't dealing with ethnology, that it is unimportant to know how many fingers a human being possesses and that it's not worth having a dialogue with one's own body when, much more simply, the world is there to discover. Others try to enter into dialogue with another mask that's performing at the same time. They remain staring at one another but neither can respond to the other. In fact a neutral mask is never able to communicate face to face with another mask. What could a neutral mask say to another mask? Nothing. All they can do is to find themselves together, facing an outside event which interests both of them.

In the course of these initial approaches to the mask, some members of the group may come up with the idea that the mask has a mystic or philosophic dimension. There are those who would like to see it as neither man nor woman. They have to be sent back to physical observation: men and women are not identical. The neutral mask is not a symbolic mask. The idea that everyone is alike is both true and totally false. Universality is not the same as uniformity. In order to clear up this confusion I suggest thoroughly realistic themes from everyday reality, even melodramatic clichés, so as to demonstrate that neutrality can also be found in these themes. An example is 'Farewell to the Boat':

A very dear friend goes on board a boat for a long journey to the other side of the world. The assumption is that you will never see him again. As the boat is leaving, you rush onto the jetty at the mouth of the harbour in order to wave him a last farewell.

This everyday theme is evoked with the people on the quayside, the mist and the ships' foghorns, but it could just as well be played out on the platform of a railway station, as a train is leaving, or anywhere else. It is not the incidental details of the exercise but the driving motor of the farewell which we are trying to bring out. In this way we can see how the farewell works, what are its dynamics. A genuine farewell is not just saying goodbye, it is an act of separation.

I am part of someone else, we have the same body, a body shared between two people, and then suddenly part of this body escapes. I try to hold it back . . . but then no! It has gone off and I am separated from part of myself. Nevertheless, I retain something inexpressible, a sort of melancholy of the body. In the end I come to terms with the farewell.

Here the motor is not linked to a particular context or character, and it is only with the neutral mask that one can reach the underlying dynamics of the situation. This farewell is not an idea, it is a phenomenon which can be observed with almost scientific precision. Getting an actor to work on this theme is an excellent way of observing him, his presence, his sense of space, seeing if his movements and his body belong to everyone, if he can find the common denominator of a gesture, one which anyone could recognise: 'The farewell of all farewells'. The neutral mask puts one in touch with what belongs to everyone, and then the nuances appear all the more forcefully. These are not nuances of character, since there is no character, but all the little differences which separate one performer from another. All bodies are different but they resemble one another through what unites them: the farewell. This collective experience points forward to the chorus, which we shall tackle at a later stage.

The fundamental journey

The great guiding theme of the neutral mask is 'The Fundamental Journey'. This journey through nature involves walking, running, climbing and jumping. The exercise is played out alone, with no interference from other actors, even if several students are performing it at the same time.

> At daybreak you emerge from the sea; in the distance you can see a forest and you set out towards it. You cross a sandy beach and then you enter the forest. You move through trees and vegetation which grow ever more densely as you search for a way out. Suddenly, without warning, you come out of the forest and find yourself facing a mountain. You 'absorb' the image of this mountain, then you begin to climb, from the first gentle slopes to the rocks and the vertical cliff face which tests your climbing skills. Once you reach the summit, a vast panorama opens up: a river runs through a valley and then there is a plain and finally, in the distance, a desert. You come down the mountain, cross the stream, walk through the plain, then into the desert, and finally the sun sets.

The image of the natural world summoned up in this exercise is one of calm, neutrality, balance. It is not a 'Boy Scout' world with a practical handbook setting a distance between man and nature. The natural world speaks directly to the neutral state. When I walk through the forest, I *am* the forest. At the summit of the mountain I feel as though my feet are in the valley and I myself am the mountain. It enables us to take the first steps towards identification. This 'Fundamental Journey', which is a major theme in my work, prepares students for work on identification of all kinds.

This journey also has symbolic overtones. The exercise allows us to introduce students to the poetic aspects of the theme: we evoke Dante's *Divine Comedy*, Shakespeare's *Tempest*, Brecht's *Resistible*

Rise of Arturo Ui. The crossing of the river can be compared to passing through adolescence to adult life, with all the movements finding their reflection in emotional feelings: the currents, the whirlpools, the waves rising and falling, washing back and forth from one bank to the other. As with all the other exercises, I give maximum encouragement to the students to fill out this journey with images which go beyond the simple geographical trip.

A second stage is to re-run the improvisation using the same theme but in extreme conditions and tempestuous weather.

> *There is a raging sea and a wave throws you up onto the beach. The sand is being swept by a rain storm. The forest is on fire. Once you are on the mountain, there is an earthquake followed by avalanches, and you slide down towards the river, which is in flood. You manage by grabbing hold of trees. Finally you reach the desert, where a sandstorm is blowing up.*

In earlier versions the 'Journey' also went through a town before reaching the desert. I preferred to dispense with the town, since it is a built environment, linked to architectural forms around which we construct a language different from the language of *mimages* [see page 109] that we use for natural movement. So we work on the town at a different stage, again going from daybreak to sunset, in a state of calm and then in a state of revolution. These improvisations in extreme conditions lead students to experience situations which they have never lived through, performing very difficult movements which they have never achieved in their own lives, enabling the body to go to the limit of its capabilities in an imagined state of urgency.

Identification with the natural world

The third phase of work with the neutral mask consists of identifications. Of course we do not mean total identification, which would be worrying, but rather playing at identification. I ask each student, with the mask on, to become the different elements of nature: water, fire, air, earth. To identify themselves with water, they play at being the sea, but also rivers, lakes, puddles, drops of water. We try to approach the dynamics of water in all their forms, from the most gentle to the most violent.

> *I am facing the sea, watching it, breathing it. My breath moulds itself to the movement of the waves and gradually the picture shifts as I myself become the sea.*

Air is principally the wind, experienced through all the objects which it sets in motion: a leaf, a sheet of corrugated iron, a rag. It consists of all kinds of turbulence, draughts, anything that blows or twirls or whirls. Earth is any substance that can be shaped and moulded, but also the tree, which I consider to be its chief symbolic image, since it is planted in the earth. It is most important for an actor to work at the tree. He must be able to achieve a body that is in balance, positively planted in the ground. An actor preparing to play Nina in Chekhov's *The Seagull* will be incapable of developing an ariel glide unless she has first acquired a basic rootedness. Fire, finally, is fire. It is the most demanding of the elements because it is nothing other than itself.

Alongside these identifications with the elements, I sometimes mention particular authors, starting with Gaston Bachelard, who analysed the materiality of the imagination: in *L'Air et les songes* [*Air and Dreams*] he has some profound things to say about the element of air. For students interested in these reflections, however, it is important that they only follow up the references after having lived the experience behind the mask, and not beforehand.

> It could be said that the furious wind is the symbol of pure anger, of anger with neither object nor pretext. The great writers of tempests . . . have loved this aspect of it: tempests without preparation, physical tragedies without cause . . . Through intimate acquaintance with images of hurricanes, one learns the nature of a furious yet vain willpower. The wind in its excess is like anger which is everywhere and

nowhere, which breeds and feeds off itself, which turns in every direction and then turns back on itself. The wind threatens and howls but it only takes on a shape when it meets dust: once visible it becomes nothing but a misery . . .

GASTON BACHELARD, L'Air et les songes, Paris:
José Corti, 1943, pp. 256–7 (trans. D.B.)

After the natural elements, work on identifications moves to different materials: wood, paper, cardboard, metal, liquids. For the actor, the objective is both to broaden his field of reference and to sense all the fine shades of difference which separate one material from another or which coexist within the same material. Substances which are doughy, unctuous, creamy, oily, all possess different dynamics. My aim is for the students to acquire a taste for such qualities, exactly as a gourmet will recognise the subtle differences between flavours. To do so involves hard work over a long period, going on to colours, lights, words, rhythms, spaces, into what we call the universal poetic awareness. At that point the neutral mask will have vanished.

Transposing

The work done on identifications has to be reinserted into the dramatic dimension. For this purpose I use the transference method, which consists of basing oneself on natural dynamics, on action gestures, on animals, on materials, using them for expressive purposes in order to achieve a better playing of human nature. The objective is to achieve a level of theatrical transposition, going beyond realistic performance.

This method offers two possible approaches. The first is to humanise an element or an animal, giving it a behaviour or a voice, relating it to other elements or animals. To give a voice to fire is to externalise distress or anger. To humanise air is to show restlessness, perpetual movement, the variable rhythm of the wind which wanders about, never settling in a particular place.

One morning the sea wakes up!
The wind is combing his hair in the bathroom!
The tree is getting dressed!
An angry person bangs on the door ... it's fire coming in!
Four trees meet up on a bench, shake hands and begin to talk.

To play a tree, to the point of making it talk and act like a human being, is to establish a poetic transposition of the character. In this case it is interesting to note that the words pronounced cannot be realistic, they too must be transposed. A special tree-language is needed which may, for example, use language similar to that of the Theatre of the Absurd. This kind of transfer allows us to discover that in the theatre words themselves, like physical gestures, must achieve a certain level of transposition.

A second possible approach is to invert the process. You begin with a human character and gradually, at particular moments of the performance, the elements or animals in which it is grounded show through. A man searching through papers, for example, will begin to show the mouse which is latent within him; another will flame with anger or love, etc. After having experienced, by means of these identifications, the greatest possible number of natural or animal dynamics, the actor (or 'author') is in a position to use these experiences, sometimes unconsciously, to feed the characters which he must act (or 'write') and to bring out some of their fundamental characteristics. He will acquire a set of references, at once very complex and very precise, as a support for future work.

The main results of this identification work are the traces that remain inscribed in each actor, circuits laid down in the body, through which dramatic emotions also circulate, finding their pathway to expression. These experiences, ranging from silence and immobility to maximum movement, taking in innumerable intermediate dynamic stages, remain for ever engraved in the body of the actor. They are reactivated in him at the moment of interpretation. It may be many years later, when an actor finds himself with a text to interpret. The text will set up resonances in his body, meeting rich deposits awaiting expressive formulation.

The actor can then speak from full physical awareness. For in truth nature is our first language. Our bodies remember!

Approach to the Arts

The universal poetic awareness

The early stages of our work at the school are not based on text, nor on any theatre tradition, oriental, Balinese, or other. Our primary reference point is simply life. So we have to be able to recognise this life through the miming body and through replay, out of which the students' imagination propels them into other dimensions and other regions. Starting from initial psychological replay, we move into the different acting levels, helped especially by mask work. In this way we can bring the great theatre traditions of *commedia dell'arte* and tragedy within the reach of second-year students. This progressive ascent is what characterises the first-year course at the school.

At the same time we set out on a second journey, down into the depths. It brings us into contact with the essence of life, which I call the universal poetic awareness. Here we are dealing with an abstract dimension, made up of spaces, lights, colours, materials, sounds which can be found in all of us. They have been laid down in all of us by our various experiences and sensations, by everything that we have seen, heard, touched, tasted. All these things are there inside us, and constitute the common heritage, out of which will spring dynamic vigour and the desire to create. Thus my teaching method has to lead to this universal poetic awareness in order not to limit itself to life as it is, or as it seems. In this way the students can develop their own creativity.

When we watch the movement of the sea, or of any element or substance such as water or oil, we are dealing with objective movements which can be identified and which arouse similar sensations in those who watch them. But there are also things which do not move and in which we can nevertheless recognise dynamic elements, such as colours, words, architecture. We can see neither the form nor the movement of a colour, nevertheless the emotion which they arouse may set us in motion – even in emotion. We try to express this particular emotion through *mimages*, through gestures which have no reference point in the real world.

Through the mimodynamic process, rhythms, spaces, forces and static objects can all be set in play. Looking at the Eiffel Tower, each of us can sense a dynamic emotion and put this emotion into movement. It will be a dynamic combining rootedness with an upward surge, having nothing to do with the temptation to give a picture of the monument (a figurative mime). It's more than a translation: it's an emotion. Etymologically, the word emotion means 'setting in motion'. In fact we constantly mime the world around us without realising it. When you are in love, your own actions instinctively mime those of the loved one. At the school we try to externalise this element instead of retaining it inside, and, for it to emerge, there must first be a recognition before this may develop into understanding and creation. In order to develop the poetic sense, whether one is an artist, writer or actor, one must feed off all these experiences.

The colours of the rainbow

We begin with colours and light. It is strange to observe that in any country, whatever its culture, the same movements appear when dealing, for example, with colours. Aside from differences of symbolism, everywhere in the world, the poetic awareness is the same: blue is Blue!

> *With the students in small groups, I call out different colours and ask them to react as rapidly as possible, without thinking, expressing the internal movement they feel. I run through all the colours of the rainbow, then they themselves choose colours which they can see in the studio, and suggest movements for them. The onlookers then try to identify the colours which have been presented.*

Improvisation

There is a tempo, a space, a rhythm which is exactly right for each colour. Together, we discover how, when a movement lasts too long or goes too far, it loses its colour. For example, the students who choose red often make explosive movements. Now, as soon as the explosion is over, the colour drains out of the movement and it turns into pure light. True red exists only just before the explosion, in the powerful dynamic tension of the instant.

When the students are performing this kind of exercise, I am particularly attentive to the quality of their movements. I can tell whether the movements arise from their own bodies or from an external image, a sort of picture postcard which they are trying to illustrate, or again if they are doing a symbolic movement, giving an external representation of the colour they are trying to describe for us. These movements have to be pruned and digressions restrained, so that the students may be taken gradually deeper into the body, closer to the true colour. This takes them beyond what can be expressed.

The pedagogical task is to isolate digressive movement without ever indicating what should be done instead. I have to create a state of uncertainty: it's up to the student to discover what the teacher already knows. The teacher must be prepared, at every moment, to question his own approach, to get back to seeing the world with freshness and innocence, to avoid imposing clichés.

Such work prepares us to approach poetry, painting and music. From analysing colours, students go on to work in a more integrated way on a whole painting. Their observation of works of art in the museums becomes the starting point for a translation in mimodynamic terms. Here again, it is not a matter of illustrating the picture, nor of explaining how they see it, but of sharing, in a direct way, the spirit of the work.

It is fascinating to observe the difference between the work on isolated colours and that done on paintings. In a pictorial work colours are displaced from their origins and set up a different dynamic. The yellow found in a Van Gogh does not move in the

49

same way as yellow on its own: it moves similarly to violet. In Chagall's paintings there is a strong contradiction between the top and the bottom, the earth and the sky. If the students try to represent one of his works, they must guard against a presentation which isolates each element: on one side the earthy aspects, on the other the characters flying through the air. It is the movement from one to the other, their way of rooting themselves or taking off, and the tension between these two elements, which is the essence of Chagall's work, and which they have to represent for us. This brings us to the heart of discussions about the nature of art.

This work is carried out by the students in groups and, when it succeeds, each student's movement can be appreciated separately, but also as part of a collective body. The next stage, for those who desire it and have a feeling for architecture, is to refine the work further, until only its structure is left. It then becomes possible to bring into play a series of abstract structures derived from different painters. In the case of Jackson Pollock, for example, the procedure is particularly interesting, for his works must be laid flat on the ground to be seen. We descend towards Pollock through successive layers in an overlapping structure which leads us into zones both deep and distressing, since they offer no foothold.

Our procedure for poetry is similar: we work on separate words before encountering poetic texts, just as in music we play with sounds before embarking on musical works.

The body of words

Words are approached through verbs, bearers of action, and through nouns, which represent a designated object. We consider words as living organisms and thus we search for the body of words. For this purpose we have to choose words which provide a real physical dynamic. Verbs lend themselves more readily to this: to take, to raise, to break, to saw, each contains an action which nourishes the verb itself. 'I saw' carries within it the dynamics of a movement. In French *le beurre* is already spread, whereas in

Improvisation

English 'butter' is always in a packet. According to the language being used, words will not all have the same relation to the body. We do lengthy work based on different languages: French, English, German, Italian, Japanese, Spanish, etc. With the word *'prendre'* [to take], for example, the French students embody the thing they are taking, closing their arms around the upper part of their bodies. They are not trying to take this or that object, but to take in a general way, to take everything, to take themselves. Germans, with *'Ich nehme'*, pick something up. The English, with 'I take', snatch. Of course, this raises the problem of translating poetry. 'I take my mother by the arm' cannot be translated as 'I pick up my mother by the arm', nor by 'I snatch my mother by the arm'. The best way to translate a poem thus seems to me to be through mimodynamics, truly putting the poem into motion in a way verbal translation can never attain.

ED È SUBITO SERA	AND SUDDENLY IT'S EVENING
Ognuno sta solo sul cuor della terra trafitto da un raggio di sole: ed è subito sera	Each is alone on the heart of the earth pierced by a ray of sun: and suddenly it's evening

Salvatore Quasimodo
(trans. D.B.)

The dynamic of this poem can be found inside each of its words: *sole* is different from 'sun', *raggio* is more energetic than 'ray', etc. In its way of naming, each language picks out a particular element. We often work on food words, since they already belong to the body, especially in French in the tradition of Rabelais, which prefers *la soupe* to *le potage*. All these words are set in motion by the students, including those who do not speak French. Curiously, they soon understand and speak our language very well, since they focus on the dynamics of the word. This suggests a tremendous opportunity for language learning.

From words, we pass on to poetry. I read the students a few poems and they choose one to work on. In small groups of three or four,

51

they set the poems in motion. This work involves finding a genuine group movement which is more than the sum of its individual movements. I suggest poems by Henri Michaux, Antonin Artaud, Francis Ponge, Eugène Guillevic, each one bearing a particular element. With Antonin Artaud it is fire, with Paul Valéry it is water when he writes of the sea and also with Ponge when he describes *des gouttes d'eau qui glissent sur les vitres un jour de pluie* ['drops of water running down window panes on a rainy day'], or again with Charles Péguy in *La Meuse endormeuse et douce à mon enfance* ['The Meuse, sweetly soporific in my childhood']. These words slip through the plain at the same slow pace as the river itself. They bear a close relation to the physical emotion of the countryside.

Apparemment,	*Outwardly,*
Tu ne fais pas de gestes.	*You make no move.*
Tu es assis là sans bouger,	*You sit there motionless,*
Tu regardes n'importe quoi,	*You stare into space,*
Mais en toi	*But within you*
Il y a des mouvements qui tendent	*Movements are tending,*
Dans une espèce de sphère	*As they stir in a kind of sphere,*
A saisir, à pénétrer,	*To grasp, to penetrate,*
A donner corps	*To give bodily shape*
A je ne sais quels flottements	*To indistinct flutterings*
Qui peu à peu deviennent des mots,	*Which slowly turn into words*
Des bouts de phrase,	*Into scraps of sense,*
Un rythme s'y met	*A rhythm begins*
Et tu acquiers un bien.	*And you acquire worth.*

Eugène Guillevic, 'Le Sorti des mots'
from *Art Poétique*, Paris: Gallimard (trans. D.B.)

On the occasion of a 'festival of poets', each student brings a poem he loves, presents it in its original language, and all follow the same approach: groups are formed to work on the text in whatever language it has been presented. This has led us to discover many foreign poets, among which are the Nordic poets, who are neglected in France. Many of the students, who never read poetry before, gain an interest in it from this experience. For me, poetry is a major source of nourishment.

Music as partner

Our approach to sounds and to music follows the same pattern. We start with work on different sounds, then move on to musical works by Bartók, Bach, Satie, Stravinsky, Berio, Miles Davis. We visualise everything that is unseen in music as if it were matter, or a moving organism. We enter into its space, we shake it, pull it, struggle with it. We embody it in order to understand it. I ask the students to recognise the music's internal movements: when it draws together, when it spirals, explodes, drops away, etc. This is not the same thing as an interpretation, which is another area. One can play entirely *against* Bartók, take up a point of view, or an opinion, see it in a particular light, which will vary with the person, their time, their culture, but before playing *against* it one must have played *with* it.

The 'Bartók Lesson' is highly structured. It is divided into several stages. Listening to the work, you must first visualise what is happening in space. Then you attempt to touch the sounds which move about. Next, you investigate whether the sounds are pushing you or pulling you, or whether it is you who are pushing and pulling them. Finally, you gradually enter a state of mutual belonging. Only after this state has been reached is it possible to choose a point of view, to be for, against or with – in other words, to create a relationship of play, for the aim is always to play with the music, just as you might play with a character. You must avoid a situation in which the music simply mimics the performance of the character or fills in the gaps, as is too often the case in the theatre.

These diverse mimodynamic procedures are essential for enriching the art of the actor. From the simple lifting of an actor's arm, the spectators must be able to sense a rhythm, a sound, a light, a colour. The challenge for the teacher is to observe with a practised eye that can distinguish, among the different gestures made, which ones are explanatory, which are formalised, and which are both truthful and poetic. Gradually, the students themselves begin to acquire subtlety in observing gestural nuances. If theatre audiences were to acquire this same subtlety of observation, they would discover untold riches. But the banality of what they are given as a rule makes this almost impossible. To train people's ability to look and see is as important as to train creative artists. It's useless giving good wine to people who can't appreciate it. That's my definition of culture: achieving a true appreciation of things.

Masks and Counter-Masks

Levels of acting

The neutral mask is unique: it is the mask of all masks. After our experiments with it, we go on to work with a great variety of other kinds of mask which we group together under the heading of 'expressive masks'. While the neutral mask is unique, the number of expressive masks is infinite. Some are made by the students themselves, others already exist, but all suggest, or rather they impose, a particular level of acting. The performer who wears an expressive mask reaches an essential dimension of dramatic playing, involving the whole body, and experiences an emotional and expressive intensity which, once again, will become a permanent point of reference for the actor.

*

The expressive mask shows a character in its broad outlines. It structures and simplifies the playing style by delegating to the body the job of expressing essential attitudes. It purifies the performance, filtering out the complexities of psychological viewpoint, and imposing guiding attitudes on the whole body. While capable of great subtlety, masked performance of this kind always depends on a basic structure which is not there in unmasked playing. That is why such work is an indispensable part of the actor's training. Whatever its dramatic style, all theatre profits from the experience an actor gains through masked performance. This is an example of teaching which does not operate directly, but through a ricochet effect, as in training for particular sports. Training to be a good shot-putter necessitates running; for a judo champion it requires body-building. Just such a sideways approach is also needed in the field of theatre. The whole school works indirectly: we never proceed in a straight line towards our students' desired goal. If someone says to me, 'I want to be a clown,' I advise him to work on the neutral mask and the chorus. If he is a clown, it will come through.

The notion of the expressive mask includes larval masks, character masks and finally utilitarian masks not originally intended for theatre use.

When we hold our 'festival of masks' each student builds a mask which we test out together. In this initial phase I ask the students not to wear their own masks. It is better for them to start by trying out those made by others, so that they can retain a certain distance from their own creation and see their masks in motion, from the outside. Some of the masks they come up with are very beautiful, but that is not enough. A good theatre mask must be able to change its expression according to the movements of the actor's body. My objective is for them to construct a mask which genuinely moves.

First-time construction of a mask can give rise to pedagogically useful mistakes. When they come to make their first mask, students often put their heads in the plaster, or build a mask to exactly the same dimensions as their own faces. As we have said, masked performance requires an indispensable distance between the mask and the actor's face. For that reason the mask must be larger (or smaller) than the face of its wearer. An expressive mask tailored to the exact dimensions of the actor's face, or, even worse, a mask moulded onto his skin, precludes playing: it is a dead mask.

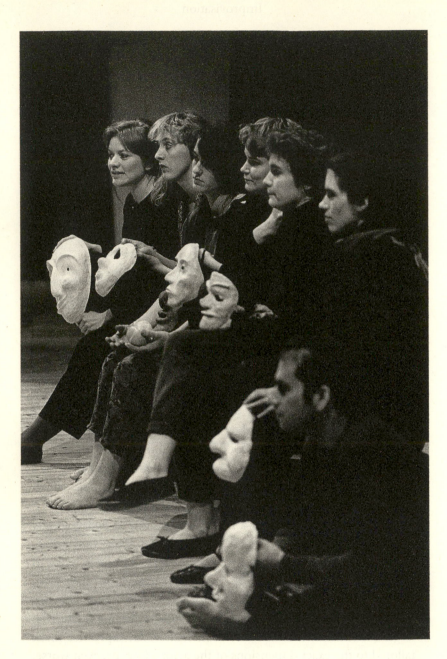

Festival of masks

There is no point in contemplating the mask for hours, with heaven knows what mystic concentration, before performing. It must be jolted into life. Very quickly, we project it into a variety of situations: 'it's happy', 'it's sad', 'it's jealous', 'it's athletic'. By pushing the mask in a number of different directions we are trying to see if it responds or not. You only really begin to know a mask when it resists this provocation. Of course a given mask does not respond to every attempt to provoke it and it only opens up in certain situations. The festival of masks allows us to do some preliminary spadework, after which I bring out the expressive masks, which represent individuals with pronounced characteristics. The students attempt to get as close as possible to these characters, to enter into the mask, without making grimaces beneath the mask, without indulging in parallel imitations imposed from outside, without looking at themselves in the mirror. To enter into a mask means to feel what gave birth to it, to rediscover the basis of the mask and to find what makes it vibrate in yourself. After this it will be possible to play it from within.

Unlike the half-masks of the *commedia dell'arte*, expressive masks are full masks, in which the actor does not speak. The characters they represent are often drawn from everyday life. Amleto Sartori's inspiration for his expressive masks came from people in the street and from the teachers at the University of Padua. True to tradition, he also drew inspiration from political figures. These masks may be somewhat exaggerated, but they are not caricatures. In performance, they must be able to manifest complex feelings. A mask which represented only the frozen expression of a single moment – that of a laugh, for example – would not be able to remain on stage for longer than a brief interlude. A good expressive mask must be able to transform, to be sad, happy, excited, without ultimately becoming fixed in the expression of a single moment. This is one of the main difficulties in its construction.

The expressive mask can be approached from two standpoints. We can take, for example, the mask known as the 'Jesuit', which has a

Jacques Lecoq wearing the 'Jesuit' mask

distorted face with one side more important than the other. On the one hand, it can be played by feeling very 'jesuitical', searching for the character's psychology, which induces particular behaviour and movements, out of which arise a given form. On the other hand, we can allow ourselves to be guided by the form itself, as it is shaped by the structure of the mask. The mask then becomes a sort of vehicle, drawing the whole body into an expressive use of space, determining the particular movements which make the character appear. Our 'Jesuit' never attacks head-on; he moves sideways, following oblique or curving movements suggested by the mask, and opening up a space for the feelings and emotions which go along with these movements. The character then arises out of the form.

Entering into the form

This way of entering into the form is encountered especially with larval masks. Invented during the 1960s for the carnival of Basel in Switzerland, these are large, simplified masks which have not quite resolved themselves into real human features. They are restricted to a large nose – a spherical protrusion, an instrument for striking or splitting. We work in two directions.

In the first place we work towards characters and situations, which are caricatured, rather as they are in comic drawings. The masks dress up in real costumes, hats, etc., as in everyday life, and we explore various realistic situations which we transpose onto the level of the masks. Secondly, we search for a dimension of the mask in animality or fantasy.

These are creatures from elsewhere which have been captured and whose reactions we shall test. Realistic characters in white coats, unmasked, organise the tests: they make the masks walk up and down, push them around with sticks, frighten them and then observe their reactions.

This research leads to the discovery of a strange, undefined and

Students improvising with larval masks

unknown population. This exploration of the incomplete body, inevitably different, opens up an imaginary realm.

Our explorations then extend to utilitarian masks: masks used by ice-hockey players, by soldiers, by skiers, etc. These are all defensive masks, designed to protect against cold or fire, light or wind. There are also masks of disguise, which facilitate spying games, secret-service games, the clandestine side of life. Care is needed, however, for although many objects can be used to make a mask, all are not equally useful. A saucepan worn as a hat with a colander adds up to nothing more than a 'gadget mask'. Among all the different possible approaches I am always on the lookout for truly dramatic masks – those which can serve as vehicles for human qualities, setting up a transposition and thus achieving a certain level of acting.

After this first experience of masked performance, I ask the performers for the opposite of what the mask appears to suggest. For example, a mask whose face seems to present 'cretin' will at first be performed as just that. The character will be foolish, timid, clumsy. Next we consider what if the character might be knowledgeable, clever, sure of himself, supremely intelligent? Here the actor is performing what we call the counter-mask, revealing a second character behind the same mask, lending it a depth which is much more interesting. In this way we discover that people's faces do not necessarily fit what they are and that for each character there is a depth of field. A third stage can be reached with certain masks: to perform, in the same character, both mask and counter-mask.

Unlike the neutral mask, the expressive mask can open the way to what I call character detours or digressions, using the same themes. When a man and a woman meet, performing in the neutral mask, their relationship is direct, going straight to the essence. It does not proceed obliquely or by detours. The man and the woman see each other, and then move towards one another in a straight line, without any obstacles troubling their relationship. With the expressive mask, the same theme might become:

The man meets the woman . . . at the post office. He is there to buy stamps, she sells them.

The situation is the same, the feelings are identical, but the characters cannot move in a straight line. Here all kinds of dramatic digressions make their appearance: they see one another, they separate; they return in a roundabout way; one approaches, the other rejects, etc. This theme could of course be played without masks, but masks facilitate breadth and focus, eliminating details so as to underline the main exchanges of attitudes. It is not the theme that is important, but the way of playing it and the level of transposition achieved. In masked performance, gestures are expanded or reduced and the eyes, so important in psychological playing, are replaced by the head and the hands, which assume great significance. This explains why real objects add so effectively to the power of the performance of the expressive mask.

Need I add that the masks referred to here have nothing to do with the symbolic masks used in oriental dance theatres, where gestures are precisely encoded? The symbolic dimension is very important in theatre, but it intervenes at a later stage: coded symbolic gestures cannot be performed until the actor has drawn nourishment from life. Certain oriental masks have extraordinary resonance, especially those from Bali, even though the Balinese perform a kind of pantomime with them. We perform differently with them, as we do with certain African masks which we sometimes use, with no attempt to research their original symbolic dimension. In fact the greatest masks of all are those of the Japanese Noh, where the slightest forward tilt of the head is sufficient to lower the eyelids and convert the gaze from outward to inward.

Characters

States, passions, feelings

All the work accomplished in the first year is moving towards one main objective: character acting. Just as they have taken on different elements, colours, insects, students must be able to take on characters, even if this involves a more difficult approach. When we begin the work on characters, I am always afraid the students will fall back on personality, in other words talk about themselves, with no element of genuine play. If character becomes identical with personality, there is no play. It may be possible for this kind of osmosis to work in the cinema, in psychological close-ups, but theatre performance must be able to make an image carry from stage to spectator. There is a huge difference between actors who express their own lives, and those who can truly be described as players. In achieving this, the mask will have had an important function: the students will have learned to perform something other than themselves, while nevertheless investing themselves deeply in the performance. They have learned not to play themselves but to play *using* themselves. In this lies all the ambiguity of the actor's work.

In order to avoid the phenomenon of osmosis, and to give us purchase on that elsewhere which we so desire, we make considerable use of animals. Each character can be compared, in part, to one or more animals. If we take a character based on the pretentiousness of the turkey, we must be sure that the turkey is indeed evident in the actor's playing. Rather than a simple encounter between actor and character, we have a relationship which is always triangular: in this case the turkey, the actor and the character.

I begin by asking students to come up with a first character freely inspired by someone observed in the street or in their own circle. They simply have to have fun being a different character. We start by defining characteristics. These are not to be confused with the

63

character's passions, nor with motivating states, nor even with the situations in which it finds itself, but consist of the lines of force which define it. Their definition must be reducible to three words. A given character might be: 'proud, generous and quick-tempered'. In this way we simplify the definition as far as possible in order to establish the basic structure which will permit the actor to play the character. With three sticks we can create a first space: a hut is already a home! Two elements would not be enough, because they would not be able to balance. For a character, just as for a house, the rules of architecture require a tripod. Once the three elements have been defined, we can begin searching for nuances: 'he is proud but brave'; 'he is quick-tempered but kind'. Little by little, the actors develop their own nuances, their own complexities, and thus their characters are built on firm foundations with a clearly defined structure.

The students come to class in character, appropriately dressed. Some of them make the journey from home in character and occasionally we do not even recognise them, so great is their physical transformation. We treat them as if they were new students and they are put into the introductory classes on movement or acrobatics. This is amusing but tiring, and so we agree on a signal which will allow them to stop playing and to relax briefly before going on. For, try as one may, characters always tend to revert towards personalities. We must remember that the students are improvising in their own words and cannot rely on the distancing effect of a text written by an author. This is why I insist on them presenting a genuine dramatic character, in other words, a character stemming from real life, not a real-life character. The difference is subtle but essential.

When they show themselves, one by one, in front of the others, we question them about their identity: their name, age, family situation, origins, work, etc., and they have to reply. After this we place them in situation so that their character can reveal itself. For, of course, character cannot be separated from situation. It is only through situation that character can reveal itself. 'Bring us to life!' is the cry of Pirandello's *Six Characters in Search of an Author*.

Place and milieu

I divide the students and their characters into broad 'families' (e.g. office workers, factory workers, academics) so as to be able to observe their behaviour. Viewed in dramatic terms, an interesting distance opens up between what the characters say when they are answering questions and what they actually do in situation. They never do exactly what they say. We set the characters in their different contexts: at home, at work, on holiday, at a party. First we place them in their own milieu before suggesting situations which disorient them or accidental situations which make them see themselves differently (also revealing them in a new light to the spectators). 'The Stalled Lift' or 'The Derailed Train' provide emergency situations in which people who would never otherwise have met quickly establish a relationship. 'The Residents' Meeting' also has rich human potential.

> Some new residents have just moved into a block of flats. They decide to invite their neighbours round in order to get to know them. Bit by bit they arrive, first the people from the flat above, then from the one below, then from next door, etc. In the course of conversation, some of them realise that they work in the same firm, but not at the same place. In the end they discover that some are office workers while others are in management. Embarrassment all around!

In this kind of situation characters emerge in a new light: sometimes timid characters display terrible authority and begin to organise things in the most surprising way. This kind of approach brings out the latent character hidden inside each person, that other, opposite character, brought to light by an unusual situation. This is an important discovery for the actor.

I have sometimes seen students take on characters which they were unable to step out of. To counter this danger, we never work for too long on the same character. We move rapidly from one to the next, rather like great film actors, who can chat about everyday matters off screen, go straight into character for a take, and then resume the same conversation.

After working on their first character, I ask the students to choose a second who should be completely different from the first. They generally alternate between one character who is closed and another who is expansive: one working-class character who is loose and relaxed, and another of higher status who is stricter, more formally dressed, with attitudes to match. Even more interesting is that these variations appear without any directive having been given.

We work on this second character in a different way: we interrogate it physically. I ask which characters 'like to be looked at', which 'nobody looks at', which 'think they are being looked at', which 'used to be looked at but aren't any longer', which 'know where they're going (are driven)', which 'don't know where they're going', etc. After this I can be more precise, asking which 'go to football matches', which 'go clubbing on Saturday nights', which 'go to museums', which 'go to sex shops'. We observe these characters in these different situations or, even more usefully, we observe their reactions when they leave them. We try to decide which places or milieux best enable the characters to reveal themselves.

These performance situations lead to technical analysis, which is a necessary stage in building a character. We emphasise the character's relationship to space: some are 'pushed from behind', others are 'pulled from in front', etc.

The third stage is when I ask them to choose two other characters, very different and complementing one another, which an actor can bring to life together. They are in a scene which involves chasing, waiting, searching and which is played around a screen.

On the stage is a screen with two panels; in front of it is open space, while the space behind is hidden. A first character arrives, looking for someone else, calls, fails to find them, goes to look behind the screen. Very rapidly, with the help of a prop or an item of costume, the actor changes character and reappears, playing the other character, pursued by the first.

The students have to build up this theme using every imaginable means. It involves playing with the illusion of multiplying characters, using changes of costume, props, voice, presentation from the front, from the back, etc. Ideally there will be a moment when they manage to show the two characters together.

Stylistic constraints

These improvisations are explored through group work, after which the students continue the work along the same lines on their own, in their *auto-cours*. I group them into 'companies' of five, asking each company to play ten characters. Anything becomes possible: separation of voices and images, multiplication of screens, etc. *L'Hotel du libre échange*[19] is a richly suggestive theme, with doors which slam, cupboards for hiding in, mistaken identities of all kinds. Here we are approaching both the virtuosity and the pleasure of play, and for me these are the most important dimensions of acting. In this exercise, as in its predecessors, my pedagogic purpose is always to oblige the students to play characters which are as distant as possible from themselves.

I conclude this introduction to characters by asking a group of actors, organised into a company, to perform a scene with sets, costumes, objects and a number of characters. Since this tends to make them spread out and take up a lot of space, I counter this tendency by a constraint: they can use only a very restricted space, measuring one metre by two. On this small, limited stage they must bring huge areas to life.

> *Two people, lost in an immense forest, search in vain for one another, then at last meet up. Physically they can be fifty centimetres apart while dramatically the distance is hundreds of metres; they can call to one another across a valley, or from the tops of hills, while all the time standing back to back.*

This exercise is performed with two actors, then with three, four or five. The upper limit is seven actors on two square metres. The exercise comes out of the cabaret tradition in which the imposition of extreme spatial constraints encourages the invention of dramatic forms. I recall the performance of a Western, complete with horses, chase sequences, saloon-bar fights, all done with tremendous verve on the tiny stage of the Rose Rouge, a famous post-war Parisian cabaret. But above all we conclude our work on characters with a reminder that the theatre must always retain its playful dimension. It is essential to have fun and our school is a happy school. Not for us tortured self-questioning about the best way to walk on stage: it is enough that it be done with pleasure.

2

Movement Technique

The second main axis of my teaching consists of movement technique. I will explain this in its own right here, although in practice it is always closely linked to performance. It comes into improvisation and into the students' own creative work throughout the course. It may serve as introduction, as support, or as an extension of the different course components. Movement technique is divided into three distinct aspects: first comes physical and vocal preparation; then dramatic acrobatics; finally, movement analysis which changes, in second year, into applied techniques relevant to the different dramatic territories.

Physical and Vocal Preparation

Giving meaning to movement

The study of human anatomy enabled me to develop an analytic method of physical preparation, directed towards expressivity and bringing into play each part of the body: feet, legs, hips, chest, shoulders, neck, head, arms, hands, getting a feel for the dramatic potential of each in turn. I have discovered, for instance, that when I move my head in ways dictated purely by geometry (side, forward, back) the result is: 'I listen', 'I look', 'I'm frightened'. In the theatre making a movement is never a mechanical act but must always be a gesture that is justified. Its justification may consist in an indication or an action, or even an inward state. I raise my arm, to indicate a place or point something out, to take an object off a shelf, or just because an inner emotion makes me feel like raising it. Indications, actions, states, these are the three ways of justifying a movement. They correspond to the three major dramatic modes: indications are related to pantomime; actions take us towards

69

commedia dell'arte; and states bring us back to drama. Whatever the actor's gesture, it is inscribed in the relationship between the actor and the surrounding space, and gives rise to an inner, emotive state. Once again, the outer space is reflected in the inner space.

Physical preparation does not aim to emulate a particular physical model, nor to impose established dramatic forms. It should assist everyone towards the fullest realisation of accurate movement. There should be no sense of the body 'getting in the way', nor of it feeding parasitically off what it should be conveying. Its foundation is dramatic gymnastics, in which every gesture, every attitude or movement is justified. I use elementary exercises, such as swinging the arms, forward or sideways bends of the trunk, swinging the legs, etc. These are all exercises generally used in physical warm-ups, to which we give meaning.

> *Arms raised and extended, a forward fall from the trunk flexes the body which bounces back up to the starting position.*

When accomplished in a precise sequence, this movement exemplifies how we proceed in all our dramatic gymnastics. We begin by carrying it out mechanically, very simply, in order to see how it goes. Next, we try to enlarge the movement to test its limits, filling the largest possible space. The third stage is to concentrate especially on two essential phases in the movement, trying to understand their dramatic dynamics. They are the starting point, with arms extended, just before the trunk collapses, and the end of the movement, with the trunk upright again and the arms in the vertical, when the body is once again extended and the movement is about to fade, imperceptibly, into stillness.

These two moments, which precede and follow the extension of the body, carry a strong dramatic charge. The state of suspension just before the beginning is part of the dynamics of risk (risk of falling) and includes a sense of anguish which emerges clearly. Conversely, the concluding suspension is one of landing, returning to a state of calm, coming gradually closer to immobility and serenity.

Next, breathing comes into play. The same movement is done on a single exhalation, covering both the fall and the rebound, inhalation coming only after the return to the immobile, extended position. Once this breath control has been mastered, I begin to suggest parallel images, which introduce a dramatic dimension into the movement. Still using the same movement, the students imagine they are looking out to sea, following the rhythm of the waves. That can lead on to imagining a ball being thrown up into the air and falling back, with the fascination exerted by the beginning and the end of the movement: what is this instant of immobility between flying up and falling back? Does the ball remain for an instant suspended in mid-air? How? In this kind of movement drama makes its appearance at the very moment of suspension. Beforehand we are simply dealing with sports. Everyone who saw Nijinsky dance says that he remained suspended in mid-air. But how?

Dramatic gymnastics also have a vocal dimension, for it would be absurd to claim that voice can be separated from body. Each gesture possesses its own sonority, or voice, which I try to help the students discover. The utterance of a voice in space shares the same nature as the execution of a gesture: just as I can throw a discus in a stadium, I can throw my voice in space; just as I can aim for a mark, I can address someone who is some distance away from me. In the waves of the sea or in the bounce of a ball, just as in any other movement, gesture, breathing and voice join to form a single movement. In this one movement, it is possible to throw out a sound, a word, a poetic sentence or a dramatic line.

The analytic approach to human movement requires an objective knowledge of anatomy on the part of the teacher. How many mistakes, some of them very dangerous for the actor, are still perpetrated by teachers who know nothing of the human body! Some ask actors to push a movement to its limits without calculating the physical danger. In reality they are loading onto the students their own anxiety about limits, and sometimes this is done quite perversely, even sadistically. They confuse the pleasure of play with the pain of exercise. An artist may choose to take on a punishing routine but the teacher must beware of forcing such things on his students.

My conception of physical preparation is in disagreement with one aspect of the movement methods recommended to many actors. Frequently, these are gymnastic methods which I call 'comforting', since their principal aim is a feeling of wellbeing for those who practise them. The various relaxation methods which are invading drama training may possibly serve to calm certain fears, or to help an individual recover their sense of personal harmony, but they never deal with the relationship to acting. For an actor, the only internal harmony that matters is that of play.

I reject the impulse which makes a teacher want to get his students to like him at any cost. This is pure demagogy. Take a naive student, make him do anything on the ground, while breathing deeply and listening to soft music, and he will be delighted. But this is often facile indulgence or convenience. There are people everywhere sailing under such flags of convenience.

Purely athletic exercises are equally insufficient for actor training. I have known actors who were extremely stiff in the gym, who nevertheless moved with wonderful suppleness on stage, and others, who were very supple in training, but who were incapable of creating an illusion. Some had acting talent, others lacked it.

Another distortion can be caused by premature apprenticeship in the formal gestures belonging to styles or codes of classical dance or of fixed dramatic forms like those of oriental theatre. Such formal gestures, often insufficiently practised, set up physical circuits in the actor's body, which then become very difficult to justify, especially when the actor is young. In these cases, actors only retain the outer, aesthetic form. Fencing, t'ai chi ch'uan and horse-riding might perhaps contribute something extra, but they can never replace the true physical education of the body of an actor who lives in the world of illusion.

Finally, exercises in group dynamics – e.g. holding hands before beginning a performance – are very nice and helpful for the group. But not for a company of professional actors. There are many directors who are keen on this kind of exercise; they are often very intelligent, but lack direct experience of physical practice, and have little understanding of the body. They are more attracted by the 'significance' of a movement than by the action itself. (I have heard that in Australia actors have their 'guru', that in the United States they are attended by a 'shrink'.) In Italy they go on stage and play. That's my idea, too.

Dramatic Acrobatics

The body's limits

Acrobatic movements appear gratuitous: they serve no purpose apart from play. They are the first natural movements of childhood. A baby emerges from its mother's body in a spiral movement; before it crawls or walks its first contact with the ground begins with a movement of the head which propels it in a sideways arc. My aim is to help the actor rediscover that freedom of movement present in children before social maturity has forced them into other, more conventional forms of behaviour.

Dramatic acrobatics begin by leaps and somersaults which become gradually more difficult, progressing to diving rolls, forward and back flips and trying to free the actor as much as possible from the force of gravity. At the same time, we work on suppleness, strength, balance (hand-stands, head-stands, shoulder-stands), on lightness (all the different jumps), but here, too, we never forget the dramatic justification for each movement. A somersault might be accidental – say I bump into an obstacle, fall and roll – while at the same time it might serve a transitional function in a play: Harlequin begins to laugh so hard that he falls into a somersault! By means of acrobatic performance, the actor reaches the limits of dramatic expression. That is why we pursue dramatic acrobatics throughout the two years, adapting them in the second year to the dramatic territories which we explore in that year. Particularly interesting are buffoonish acrobatics consisting of violent falls and catastrophic collapses of whole pyramids made possible by the padded costumes worn by *bouffons*.

Juggling complements the acrobatic approach. It begins with one ball, then two, three, four, five or more. More importantly, it progresses to everyday objects such as plates or glasses, and is ultimately built into a sequence of dramatised play (the restaurant, the shop, etc.). Next come fights: slapping and being slapped, kicking, hair-pulling, nose-twisting, group fights which give the greatest possible illusion of violence without ever being real, of course. The actor who is slapped, or whose hair is pulled leads the game, and creates the illusion. Here is an essential law of theatre which we have already observed: reaction creates action.

Finally, objects are added: the flying chair, the table you roll on, etc. We also work on assistance and safeguards to acrobatic movement, preventing the actor from falling. In a backwards flip, for example, a hand placed in the small of the back can help the actor to complete the movement without danger. This supporting role, is, in turn, dramatised: I bend down to pick something up, someone else rolls on my back, I stand up to see what is happening and in doing so I help them to complete their jump! The technical mastery of all these acrobatic movements, falls and jumps, has in reality a single aim: to give greater freedom to the player.

Movement Analysis

Movement analysis applied to the human body and to nature, charting the economy of physical actions, is the foundation of the school's physical work. The things I had practised as an athlete naturally carried over into action mime. When I started, I used Georges Hébert's 'natural method', which analyses movement under eleven categories: pulling, pushing, climbing, walking, running, jumping, lifting, carrying, attacking, defending, swimming. These actions lay down circuits in the human body, through which emotions flow. Feelings, states and passions are expressed through gestures, attitudes and movements similar to those of physical actions. Young actors have to be aware of how the body can 'pull' or 'push' so that, when the need arises, thay can express the different ways in which a character can 'pull' or 'push'. The analysis of a physical action does not mean expressing an opinion, but acquiring physical awareness which will form an indispensable basis for acting.

The foundation: natural everyday movements

I begin by analysing the movements of the human body based on three natural movements which occur in everyday life: undulation, inverse undulation and eclosion.

I discovered undulation as the principle of all physical effort, in the sports stadium. It was on the stage of the theatre at Grenoble that I discovered eclosion. And it was at the rue du Bac, the first home of the school, that I perfected inverse undulation, discovering the meaning of conflict and character. This is how I identified the three principles of bodily movement, and with them the three main pathways of my teaching method.

Beyond their simple basis in physical movement, these three principles also provide analogous pathways to those of masked performance. Eclosion corresponds to the neutral mask; undulation to the expressive mask in its first image; and inverse undulation brings us back to the counter-mask. These movements sum up three dramatic positions: being with; being for; being against.

Undulation is the human body's first movement, the one underlying all locomotion. Fishes in water undulate to achieve forward motion. Snakes in the grass also undulate. A child on all fours undulates as well, and humans in the upright position continue to undulate. If you film people coming out of the metro,

Undulatory movement

Undulation

Eclosion

analysis of their movements will show that they rise and fall: they follow an undulating line. Any undulating movement progresses from a point of leverage to a point of application. Undulation takes its leverage from the ground and effort is gradually transmitted to all the parts of the body until it reaches the point of application. A similar transmission can be seen when you blow on water and a wave moves almost imperceptibly. When a human being walks, this undulation is found in the pelvis. The pelvic area draws the rest of the body into a natural double undulation: one is lateral, like a shark's, and the other is vertical, like a dolphin's. Undulation is the driving force behind all physical effort manifest in the human body, which comes down to pushing/pulling (see pages 85–7).

Inverse undulation is the same movement, but inverted. Instead of starting from the leverage of the feet on the ground, it starts from the head, which initiates the movement by taking its lead from something outside me that sets me in motion. The image of the bird can help to realise this movement:

There is a bird in front of me and I watch it from a distance. It rises vertically above my head and I follow it with my eyes. It is about to fly down and I step back. It is down and I watch it on the ground. Then it flies off to the horizon.

In a movement like this, which starts from the head, the whole body is mobilised. The mode employed is one of dramatic indication. Whereas undulation is a voluntary action, initiating movement from one point to another, inverse undulation always expresses dramatic reaction. In reality, all drama inverts the techniques of movement.

Undulation and inverse undulation share four main body-positions as the movement unfolds: inclined forwards, drawn up to its full height, inclined backwards and hunched. I ask the students to adopt these positions one after the other and then, in the course of this physical progression, to experience passing

77

through the different ages: infancy, adulthood, maturity, old age. The body in forward position, back arched, head thrust forward, suggests an image of childhood or the figure of Harlequin. The vertical position, with the body upright, takes us back to the neutral mask, to the mature adult. The autumn of life, or digestive phase, makes us incline backwards from the vertical axis. We fall back into retirement. Finally old age hunches us up so that we become, once more, like a foetus.

Balanced between the two preceding movements, eclosion opens up from the centre. It starts from a crouched position down on the ground, the body occupying the smallest possible space, and opens up to finish on the 'high cross' position, upright, legs together and arms extended above the horizontal. Eclosion consists in moving from one position to the other without a break and with each segment of the body following the same rhythm. Arms and legs arrive simultaneously at the extended position, no one part of the body preceding another. The difficulty is to find exactly the right balance and an unobstructed dynamic. Too often the upper part of the body reaches the end before the arms, simply because more attention is being given to it. Eclosion is a global sensation which can be performed in both directions: expanding or contracting.

After having worked on each of the basic movements, I suggest treatments for these exercises. By treatment, I mean a set of variations whose purpose is to explore different adaptations of the movement. After the simple gesture has been analysed, I manipulate it in different ways so as to help the students to expand their expressive field. The main principles of technical treatments are: expansion and reduction, equilibrium and respiration, disequilibrium and progression. These are applied to all the basic analytic movements and then to all the physical actions, so that in the end they can be adapted for performance itself, and for feelings.

We always begin by expanding the movement to its maximum in order to find its spatial limits, taking it to the limits of balance (i.e. just before over-balancing). Maximum expansion of undulation takes us to a point of balance in space, both in front and behind. After this, we take the opposite course, reducing the same movement to the point where it is almost imperceptible from outside. We have reached the opposite limit, which consists simply in respiration, in apparent immobility.

Equilibrium and respiration are the extreme limits of all movement applicable to the performance of the actor. In improvisation work, we generally start from a simple situation, then expand it to the maximum, increasing our feelings to their limit before reducing the situation again. Starting from a smile, we try to laugh until we burst, before we return to an intermediate laugh. An actor who has practised this exercise and experienced the upper limit of the laugh will be free to react with great subtlety and vividness in psychological drama. The whole range of laughter will be present in his performance. In this procedure we move from expressionism to impressionism, from the play of the whole body to the play of the perceiving eye.

Finally, we explore the situation beyond its limits. Pushing a movement beyond the point of balance provokes imbalance, we begin to fall, and in order to avoid this fall, we invent locomotion. We move forward. This law of physical movement is no less valid for the stirring of the emotions.

It is important for actors to begin by playing very large, so as to sense the lines of force, the broad outlines of the character. There will be time, later, to find the nuances in a more intimate way of playing. Psychological acting ought to be the result of a performance that has been through maximum expansion in space. I am struck by the fact that certain great actors, who can give intimate performances of great power, began in a different dimension: Jean Gabin,[20] for instance, was in music-hall before he became an actor, as we know. This idea is very different from the approach found in many actor-training programmes, where students are expected to begin by playing 'small', and then gradually enlarge their performance. This approach is all in vain! That is when their playing becomes external, 'hammy'.

79

The samurai

The table

The grand Harlequin no. 1

The forward feint

The hip opening

The mirror hip opening

The rolling forward feint

The grand Harlequin no. 2

The table

The samurai

Bringing out attitudes

When we begin to work with the neutral mask, we need to get the body to produce a series of attitudes which will provide a structure for movement going beyond natural gestures. I use the word attitude to convey a powerful moment of stasis, isolated within a movement. It is a moment of stillness which can be placed at the beginning, at the end or at a key point. When you push a given movement to its limit, you reveal an attitude.

I organise this work around the 'nine attitudes', an ordered progression which I ask the students to carry out in sequence. This exercise gives rigour to the pelvis, the trunk and the head, thus going against their natural movement. Using an artificial approach (as in all transposition into artistic form, e.g. neutral mask, *commedia dell'arte*) we play against nature the better to depict it. Once the sequence has been completed, and the attitudes mastered, treatments are once again introduced: expansion/reduction, equilibrium/respiration, and then the dramatic justifications, which we leave the students to discover for themselves (I look, I turn round, etc.). In addition, all kinds of variations are introduced, especially variations of breathing. You only need to apply a counter-respiration to a movement for its justification to change. The example of 'The Farewell' is the best one to illustrate this:

> In a standing position, I raise my arm to the vertical to wave goodbye
> to someone.

If this movement is made while breathing in as the arm is raised, and then breathing out as it falls back, the sense of a positive farewell results. If you do the opposite, raising the arm on the out breath, and letting it fall as you breathe in, the dramatic state becomes a negative: I don't want to say goodbye, but I am obliged to do so! Another possibility: breathe in, hold your breath, then do the movement, and only breathe out once it is completed, which gives rise to the Fascist salute. Finally, the opposite is also possible: breathe out, then do the movement before breathing in again.

Perhaps there is a bayonet at my back, forcing me to do it! All these nuances of breath control are applied to the nine attitudes and have a profound effect on the dramatic justifications which are produced.

The nine attitudes and their dramatic justifications are interesting because of their contradictions. 'The great Harlequin', a movement pulling the pelvis back, may equally well suggest reverence, fear or stomach-ache. There is never one single justification: its opposite is often equally possible. All the main attitudes bring multiple possibilities, and this makes them eminently dramatic, as well as being very valuable in a pedagogic perspective. It is up to the students to strike out, and discover all the variants, especially in the transitions from one attitude to the next. It is up to them to discover the importance, for an actor, of retaining the underlying structuring principles of these attitudes, even in their smallest, most intimate versions.

The notion of the attitude is evident in the work of every great actor, whatever their style of theatre, for in fact theatre audiences demand attitudes which they can follow. Fuzzy gestures are undesirable in the theatre, except for when attitudes have become excessively stereotyped and we have to fight to inject new life into them. An example was the experience of The Living Theatre[21] at the end of the 1960s: their cries and screams shattered the old codes, but after that much-needed revolt, they had to rebuild. It is just such a discovery that I hope my students will make, starting from the simplest, most natural gestures, and ending up with the most elaborate theatre. For all great theatre is highly structured.

Researching the economy of physical actions

Action mime provides our basis for analysing the physical actions of humans. It consists in reproducing a physical action as closely as possible, with no transposition, miming the object, the obstacle, the resistance. For this I make use of labouring trades: the

Climbing

Lifting/Carrying

Bell-ringing

Climbing over the gate

boatman, the man working with a shovel or a pick, the wood-cutter, or I use sports exercises, such as pull-ups or weightlifting. Action mime also copies the handling of objects: opening a suitcase, closing a door, taking a cup of tea.

Avoiding psychological explanations, we research the most economical form of a physical action, so that it can serve as a reference point. As before, these movements are first analysed from a technical point of view, before being pushed to their maximum, and then reduced to discover their dramatic content, so that we can escape from the atrophied form known as 'mime'.

To avoid falling into pure technique, or virtuosity for its own sake, we never stop at the analysis of separate movements, but fit gestures into dramatised sequences, having a beginning and an end. The sequence called 'The Wall', comprising fifty-seven very precise attitudes, allows for an overall sequence of movements.

You are in a town, being chased; you hide beneath an archway at the end of an alley. Your pursuer passes by without seeing you. Your only way out is by climbing over a wall, on the other side of the street. You rush to it, climb and jump down on the other side. Unfortunately, he has seen you and is already there waiting for you!

This sequence is analysed, attitude by attitude, and the students work on each one in turn. Only when they have a good knowledge of all of them can they free themselves sufficiently to find how best to play them and discover the rhythm of the sequence. The body must be disciplined in the service of play, constrained in order to attain freedom.

The students are then asked to work on the same sequence in their *auto-cours*, composing a group ballet, in which the meaning of the actions and their dramatic dimension is hidden, leaving only the movements themselves, performed to music. A number of rules can be worked out: a movement can be repeated several times, singly or by the whole group, synchronised or not.

Action mime shows us that everything a person does in their life

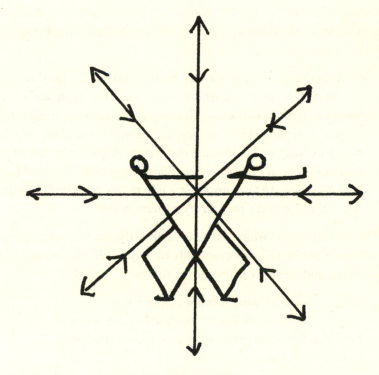

The rose of effort

can be reduced to two essential actions: 'to pull' and 'to push'. We do nothing else! These actions include the passive 'I am pulled' and 'I am pushed' and the reflexive 'I pull myself' and 'I push myself' and can go in many different directions: forwards, to one side or the other, backwards, diagonally, etc. I call this the rose of effort.

It comprises a multi-directional space which can be adapted to all human movements, whether physical or psychological, whether a simple movement of the arm or an all-consuming passion, a movement of the head or a profound desire, everything brings us back to pull/push.

> *Harlequin refuses to go to the war. Everyone tries to convince him. At first he gives a categorical refusal, insists, but then gradually allows himself to be persuaded and ends up agreeing. Everyone is delighted, but then he retracts. At last he makes up his mind to go alone, into the front line, ready to kill anything that moves. People try to make him understand that it's dangerous, that he could just as well stand back from the action. All to no avail. He is now the one in control, dragging everyone along, while they all try to restrain him.*

The driving force which structures this theme (the reversal of situation) can be reduced essentially to 'pull/push' with a variation of levels, and then an inversion of forces:

> *I urge someone to move forward ... he refuses*
> *I go in front and pull him by the hand ... he resists*
> *I pull harder ... he pulls me in the opposite direction*
> *I pull even harder ... he gives in*
> *He comes with me ... he overtakes me*
> *He drags me after him ... I resist*
> *I let him go ... he escapes*

Three main directions are contained within the rose of effort: verticals, horizontals, diagonals. The actions of someone rowing a boat (standing or sitting) or sawing a log are horizontal. They come and go between push and pull. Bell-ringing, climbing, lifting, carrying, Ancient Greek discus-throwing, are vertical actions.

Finally, diagonal movements can be found in the wood-chopper or the boatman with a punt-pole.

These three movements refer back to three different dramatic worlds. Horizontal 'pull/push' corresponds to 'you and me'. This is dialogue as found in the *commedia dell'arte* or the clown routine. Vertical movement situates man between heaven and earth, between zenith and nadir, in a tragic event. Tragedy is always vertical: the gods are on Mount Olympus. *Bouffons* are also vertical, but in the other direction: their gods are underground. As for the diagonal, it is sentimental, lyrical, it flies off and we cannot tell where it will come down. This is the terrain of the broad emotions of melodrama.

Every dramatic territory can be assigned its precise spatial situation, and the physical movements we study, from the simplest to the most complex, take their place in these dramatic dimensions. I love, I pull. I hate, I push.

Analysing the dynamics of nature

After analysing the movements of the human body, we go on to analyse the movements of nature: elements, materials and animals are looked at in the same way as we did for identifications [see page 43]. Movements found in the course of improvisation are reviewed from a technical point of view, trying to bring out the different parts of the body involved.

The four elements (water, fire, air and earth) are approached through their different manifestations. When it comes to water, we have to discover ponds, and lakes, and rivers, and the sea. For example, we observe the movement of a body in relation to the sea: it is lifted by the water, thrown back by the waves, dragged into a sidelong struggle in its desire to penetrate. Water is a moving, resisting force, which can only be experienced by struggling with it. It is only from the pelvis that this overall sensation can be transmitted to the whole of the body. We emphasise the involvement of the pelvis so as to avoid arm- or hand-gestures which would tend to 'signify' the sea without experiencing it.

Fire is born from within. It flows from breathing and from the diaphragm. In fire, two movements can be distinguished: combustion and flame. We begin with combustion, at the level of the diaphragm, and then gradually discover the rhythms of fire, discovering very quickly that its dramatic justification lies in anger. Flames only come at a second stage, after which we can work on other interesting images, like boiling water for instance.

Air is found through flight. Running across the room, arms outstretched like a glider, we can sense the possibility of getting leverage on the air, which is not a vacuum but an element that can give support. The whole body is drawn in. Air at its most extreme, in the form of 'the four winds', affects human beings, pushing and pulling them. But humans can also affect the air, moving it about with a fan.

Finally we work on earth, in the form of clay which we can compress, smooth, stretch. Here, the sensation begins from the hands, before spreading to the whole of the body. While it is easy to experience sensations which start from the hands, it is also important to involve the rest of the body, the pelvis, the solar plexus, in a confrontation with the imagined clay. Starting from the earth, which I manipulate, I gradually turn into the manipulated clay.

The main distinguishing features of materials are their passivity and the fact that they are displayed largely through their reactions. Their movements can only be analysed once they have been attacked. We have to throw, crumple, pound, tear or shatter a material before we can observe its reaction. In the process, it is important not to confuse the material with the object made from it. When you throw a wooden bowling ball on the ground, it's not the wood rolling, it's the ball. A ball made of lead will roll differently but will still roll. Now, what interests us is the wood or the lead. To facilitate technical analysis, I have classified the different types of material.

First there are those which settle and remain inert when you act on them: lead thrown to the ground, clay which splats, wire which is bent. Once attacked, these materials no longer alter their shape. The dramatic analogy might be: 'I have said my say – there's no going back.'

On the other hand, elastic materials, once stretched, are nostalgic for a return to their initial shape, even though they may not quite succeed. There are innumerable variants: rubber, elastic, various fibres. The more you pull them, the more they suffer fatigue, reducing their ability to return to their original shape. Dramatically speaking, the dynamics of nostalgia and fatigue are very interesting.

Then come the marks, bruises, creases and folds which you can observe in crumpled paper. Paper also tries to recover its initial shape, but cannot do so with the ease of elastic materials. This introduces the tragic dimension, which emerges in different ways according to the different materials used. The tragedy of newspaper is not the same as that of paper used to wrap flowers; the drama of greaseproof paper used by the butcher is not the same as that of recycled writing paper. The indelible creases in the paper suggest the innumerable scars which speak to us all of our nostalgia for paradise lost.

Finally, we come to breakages, splinterings, cracked glasses, shattered window panes, explosions. Here more than anywhere else, perhaps, we are looking at ourselves, at the variety of our internal cracks and divisions.

Materials may be altered by cold and heat as well as by being physically attacked. Things that melt, evaporate or solidify are rich in dramatic analogies, as can be seen from common turns of phrase: 'his anger melted', 'that man is like a block of ice', 'she froze', 'the meeting broke up', 'I was ruffled by what he said', etc. We take these expressions literally, embodying the words.

Cookery is a happy hunting ground for analysis and performance, working on the processes through which food is put. What hits the pan first: the yolk or the white of the egg? Every student has to go and cook an egg, for real, before performing, so that they can see that the yolk falls first, dragging the lighter white behind it. After that we go on to the way it spreads across the pan and the different stages of cooking: gelatinous wobbling, little trembles caused by the first heat, gradual solidification, the first burned bits, carbonisation. In our analysis, we follow the whole Passion of the egg, from when it is laid to when it is served as an omelette.

Lastly, the technical analysis of materials moves from their manipulation to the materials themselves. When we come to oils, the students start by being the bottle of oil inside which, through pelvic movements, they can feel the dynamics of the enclosed oil, before they pour it out onto the ground and, at that moment, themselves become the oil. We observe the way the oil pours from the bottle, then the way it spreads out unstoppably over the ground. It is all a matter of rhythm and fluidity, something very difficult to achieve when your elbows and knees hit the ground, reminding you that you have a skeleton. The technique is to restrain the movement, not to allow it to go too quickly, so as to prolong it as far as possible, both in time and space.

Another person's body can also be treated as if it were a material: twisting a body, like a metal bar, crumpling it like paper. An actor grasps his partner, crumples him up and throws him on the floor, then the partner continues on his own, showing the reaction of the paper as it straightens out again. This kind of exercise requires precision from both performers, not only from the one who acts but also the one who reacts, to ensure that the resistance of the material has real continuity, from the start to the end of the movement. A similar exercise can be tried with a balloon: one student 'inflates' the other, bit by bit, varying his breathing rhythms, then suddenly lets him shoot into the air or, perhaps, pierces him so that he bursts. Here again is an exercise for two players who must discover the ability to attend to and react to one another, which is a necessary preparation for all acting.

Movement Technique

The rain, in the courtyard where I watch it falling, comes down at very varied speeds. In the middle, it is a fine discontinuous curtain (or network), an inexorable but relatively slow cascade of doubtless lightweight droplets, a sempiternal precipitation with little force, an intense fraction of pure meteorology. Closer to the walls to right and left, heavier, separated drops are falling with more sound. Here they seem the size of a grain of wheat, there as big as a pea, elsewhere almost as large as a child's marble. On bars and window-ledges, the rain runs horizontally, while on the underside of the same obstacles it hangs like hollowed-out humbugs. Over the entire surface of a small zinc-covered roof the eye follows it streaming down in a thin sheet, the shimmering ripples caused by varying currents flowing over the imperceptible undulations and bumps of the roof-covering. From the adjoining gutter, where it babbles like a hollow stream on a gentle slope, it falls all at once in a perfectly vertical but roughly plaited trickle until it reaches the ground, where it breaks up and splashes out in shimmering splinters.

Each of its forms has its own particular speed and to each speed corresponds a special sound. The whole is intensely alive, a complex mechanism, both precise and haphazard, like a clock whose spring is the weight of a given mass of cascading vapour.

The sound as these vertical trickles hit the ground, the gurgling of the gutters, the tiny gong beats, all this multiplies and reverberates into a concert with no monotony, and some delicacy.

When the spring is unwound, some of the cogs continue to turn for a while longer, going more and more slowly, until the whole machinery comes to a stop. Then if the sun comes out again everything is soon wiped away, the brilliant apparatus evaporates: it has rained.

Francis Ponge, 'La Pluie' in *Le Parti pris des choses*,
Paris: Gallimard, 1942 (trans. D.B.)

At the end of these exercises the students will have experienced every possible nuance, both between different materials and within each one of them: the special properties of different oils, vapours, papers, metals, woods, etc. Material dynamics become a language which will be useful to them throughout their artistic careers. They will be able to say: 'You're too oily; you're not leaden enough; be a diamond!' This language of analogy is both rich and precise and goes beyond any psychological approach. If a stranger comes into the room while we are working on materials, ignorant of what we are doing, he may think we are performing a tragedy. A crumpled piece of paper, a sugar-lump which crumbles in liquid, are examples of movements with a powerful tragic content. The tragedy of materials comes from their passive character. They submit!

Studying animals

The analysis of animal movement brings us closer to the study of the human body and helps with character creation. Broadly, animals resemble us, having bodies, feet, heads. This makes them easier to approach than materials or the four elements. Research on animal bodies begins with their purchase on the ground: how do they stand? What is their contact with the ground, and how does it differ from ours? We discover hooves which trot, making only brief contact with the ground (reminiscent of women in high heels), the flat feet of plantigrades (e.g. bears); the webbed feet of ducks who walk with a rolling gait (like Charlie Chaplin); the feet of flies which work like suction pads, sticking to the floor, etc. I encourage students to imagine that the floor of the room is burning hot, like a sandy beach under the midday sun, obliging them to discover the dynamics of that particular kind of walk. Here we move directly from analysis to performance.

Next we investigate animal attitudes. What are the attitudes available to a dog? On all fours, sitting up, lying down, ears pricked, etc. Each student comes up with a few attitudes, out of which the group settles on fifteen or so. Some animals provide cases of slow motion: the chameleon is one: he can move without a tremor passing from legs to head. Ideal for a spy! The movement from relaxation to being on the alert is a special element in animal dynamics. A dog can instantly go from defence to attack, from sleep to the alert. Once analysed, all these dynamics can be built into the performance of character.

Through work on animals, I have gradually come to define what I call animal gymnastics. Work on flexibility of the spine is done by analogy with cat movements, movements of the shoulder blades refers to lions and tigers, elongation of the spinal column is done with reference to meerkats standing guard in the desert. In this kind of gymnastics, we are not attempting to perform exceptional feats, but rather to discover the elementary, organic movements of the animals. For work on neck- and head-movements, reference to dogs is particularly useful.

A man and his dog play with a little ball.

This game, played out by two students, develops their speed of response, mainly involving head movements. In fact a dog hardly moves his eyes, moving his head instead, which leads us straight on to masked playing. The students are already using the movements called for in masked performance, though they don't yet know it.

Locomotion is an important aspect to be observed in animal movement. In particular we deal with quadrupeds (walking on four feet), but we also touch on reptile crawling (undulation at its most basic), the flight of birds and the swimming of fish. Once again: earth, air and sea. We walk on all fours, we gallop, we trot, we gambol, etc., all movements which are particularly difficult for human beings to accomplish with ease.

At the start of this work, some students reject contact with the ground; they avoid supporting the whole weight of the body on their arms, they try to use just their fingertips. In so doing, they are trying to maintain balance on their legs, only pretending to walk on all fours. Not until they meet the ground on its own terms, and make full contact with it, can they progress.

Real observation of animals is essential here. I can soon tell which students have cats and which don't, which have observed insects and which are just imagining them. The first ones act, the others demonstrate. They have to go to the zoo to observe and to analyse, however difficult it may be: the walk of a giraffe or a bear are extremely complex and cannot easily be embodied.

The laws of motion

Movement analysis gives rise to a few common laws of motion, which I sum up as follows:

1. There is no action without reaction.
2. Motion is continuous, it never stops.
3. Motion always originates in a state of disequilibrium tending towards equilibrium.
4. Equilibrium is itself in motion.
5. There is no motion without a fixed point.
6. Motion highlights the fixed point.
7. The fixed point, too, is in motion.

These principles can be elaborated by examining the results of the ceaseless play between forces in equilibrium and in disequilibrium: oppositions (in order to stand upright, man must oppose gravity), alternations (day alternates with night as laughter with tears), compensations (carrying a suitcase in the left hand forces one to compensate by lifting the other arm). These notions may appear abstract, but they are, physically, very concrete on the stage, and are central to my teaching. They are particularly valuable in production, involving the whole art of knowing how to situate oneself in relation to a fixed point, in a given situation, defined by a relationship with another person. If everyone on stage moves simultaneously, the sense of movement disappears for want of a fixed point, becoming incomprehensible and impossible to make sense of. Actors have to be able to place themselves with reference to others, in a clear relationship of listening and response.

Paradoxically, this work on movement, evidently so applicable to performance and production, should be even more useful to the writer. Whatever the themes dealt with, the ideas expressed, the stories or styles employed, it is essential for playwriting to be structured from a dynamic point of view. In particular, it must have a clear beginning and an end, for any movement which fails to end has no true beginning. The sense of an ending is essential.

3

The Students' Own Theatre

Auto-Cours and investigations

Auto-cours is the name we give to sessions of an hour and a half which take place each day, when groups of students work on their own, without direct supervision by teachers. They prepare a performance based on a theme which I suggest, and present their work in front of the whole school at the end of each week. This is their own theatre. Their work is linked to the subjects improvised during classes. When we work on silent psychological play, the *auto-cours* deals with this aspect of the work, and it's the same when we are dealing with the neutral mask, with expressive masks, etc.

The first theme I suggest is extremely simple. I ask them to form groups of between five and seven people, and to develop a performance on the theme of four words: 'A place, an event'. Faced with an assignment of such simplicity, they are sometimes lost. 'What should we be doing?' they ask. I don't have an answer. 'How long should it last?' As long as it takes to do something interesting! The only thing to do is to remain silent and something will happen – as in the theatre.

A second main theme involves the whole class performing together. Their task is to represent the life of a square in a village or small market town in France from dawn to nightfall. The students have to feel, and make us feel, the rhythmic progression of life in the course of one complete day, carrying out all the actions which could really take place: cleaning, encounters in the street, shopping, meals, the Mass, the market, etc. This group experience of replay is especially interesting in bringing together, in less than twenty minutes (more is always too long), all the underlying dynamics of one day in our lives. We realise what are the key times for collective life: the hour when the whole of France stops for the midday meal, the time when work gradually picks up again, dusk, night life, nocturnal solitude, etc. This performance is developed over two weeks, with a preliminary version at the end of the first week.

A third theme, that of 'The Exodus', was very poignant in the post-war years and is now finding new echoes. I suggest this theme alongside work on masks. The students develop and rehearse without masks, and then perform wearing masks. All types of exodus appear: migration from the countryside to the towns, refugees fleeing war and bombs, etc. In this way the students can project contemporary concerns onto an imaginary realm which is of global significance. My comments deal only with the structure of the performance and the dramatic development of the improvisation. Everything must be clear to the spectators. This is why we also try to encourage the students' search for a way of writing, and a language.

At the end of the year, *auto-cours* make way for investigations. Students choose a place and a milieu, somewhere which is part of everyday life, but not familiar to them. They become part of it and observe it for four weeks. Some students have, for example, spent several weeks at the hospital of the Hôtel-Dieu in Paris, feeding the patients and assisting the doctors, others have joined in the life of a fire station. It is not a matter of conducting a journalistic enquiry, which would amount to mere observation filled out with a few conversations with the people there. Instead, it involves genuine integration into a live working environment, with the aim of experiencing what happens there as full participants. Basing themselves on this lived experience, they develop a short perform-ance, using the theatrical devices which seem best suited to putting across what they have felt. The results of this work are presented in public on open evenings.

Unlike improvisation work, which deals mainly with acting, the

Jacques Lecoq and his staff reflecting on a student presentation

work done in the *auto-cours* emphasises production, playwriting, and also the necessity of collaborative work in the theatre. At the start of the first year the students do not know each other, they are very nice and polite with one another. Over the course of time, as their involvement heightens, their relationships change, opening the way to every conceivable kind of conflict. Unlike short courses, after which everyone kisses, sheds tears and promises to meet again, the school is a place of struggle, of tension and crises, out of which creativity is sometimes stimulated. Occasionally a student will come to me and say: 'They won't play with me!', to which I have only one reply: 'Well, play with them!' By placing oneself at the service of others, one discovers an important dimension of theatre work. Through these tensions and crises, they begin to experience life as part of a company. The third stage is more tranquil. After a certain time, the students know one another well, they choose who to be with, and the tensions diminish. I suggest, nevertheless, that they should not always work with the same companions but allow themselves to be stimulated by contact with other personalities as well.

Finally, the *auto-cours* quite rapidly leads to the emergence of different roles in the creative process: students discover strengths as directors, authors, actors. The person who becomes powerful in the group is not necessarily the one who most wanted to take the lead; sometimes an unassuming personality reveals a powerful presence and is, in effect, singled out by his colleagues. All such internal group dynamics emerge in the course of this type of work. It is good for future actors to discover these realities in the course of their time at the school.

III

THE ROADS
TO CREATIVITY

Clown performance by second-year students

Geodramatics

At the end of the first year, about a third of the students are chosen to go on into the second year. The selection process may be a difficult, sometimes a painful one, and we are not infallible. But we try to be as fair as possible, weighing up the actor without wounding the person, and our choices make no claim to predict what students may go on to do. The main criterion for selection is the actor's capacity for play. This does not mean that, in their future lives, all will choose to become actors. Some will follow other paths, into writing or directing. But the dramatic terrain explored in the second year can only truly be experienced through performance when developed to its highest level, so students have to prove they have great qualities in this area. A true understanding and knowledge of theatre inevitably requires a profound experience of play.

In the course of the first year we shall have planted the roots, enriched the soil, turned over the earth. We shall have completed three journeys: first, the observation and rediscovery of life as it is through replay, thanks to the freedom conferred by the neutral mask; second, we shall have raised the levels of playing, by means of expressive masks; finally, we shall have explored the poetic depths of words, colours, sounds. The first year will have built up a very precise body of work which will remain as our point of reference. Come what may, a tree is still 'The Tree', and we shall need to continue our practice of observing it.

The second year, however, is very different. It does not form a logical continuation of the first, but a qualitative leap towards another dimension: geodramatic exploration of huge territories with one single objective: dramatic creation.

We start with physical and gestural languages. Next we embark on the grand emotions of melodrama, followed by the human comedy of *commedia dell'arte*. The second term is devoted to *bouffons*, then tragedy and its chorus and finally to mystery and its madness. Clowns and comic varieties (burlesque, eccentric, absurd, etc.) occupy the third term. The year begins in tears, moves through the experience of collaborative chorus-work and ends in solitude and laughter.

This sequence we work through in the second year explores the different facets of human nature. Melodrama involves us in grand emotions and the pursuit of justice. In *commedia dell'arte* we discover the human comedy: little wheelings and dealings, petty deceptions, hunger, desire, the rage for life. *Bouffons* caricature the real world, underline the grotesque aspects of all hierarchies of power. Tragedy evokes a grand popular chorus and the destiny of the hero. Mystery questions everything that remains incomprehensible, from birth to death, the before and the after, the devil who provokes both the gods and our imaginations. Lastly, the clown has the freedom to make people laugh, by showing himself as he is, entirely alone.

But there is always a danger that students will rely on the cultural references which come with these dramatic territories. Each of us has his own way of imagining the past, the pictures he has seen, the books he has read, his own particular clichés too. Everyone claims to know what melodrama was, what *commedia dell'arte* and tragedy were, but who can say how tragedies were really performed in Ancient Greece, or *commedia dell'arte* in Renaissance Italy? No reading of reference books can substitute for creative work, renewed each day in the school. Beyond styles or genres, we seek to discover the motors of play which are at work in each territory, so that it may inspire creative work. And this creative work must always be of our time.

My method aims to promote the emergence of a theatre where the actor is playful. It is a theatre of movement, but above all a theatre of the imagination. In the course of the second year, we shall not just aim to see and to recognise reality, but to imagine it, to give it body and form. Our method is to approach the 'territories of drama' as if theatre were still to be invented.

We emphasise the poetic vision in order to develop the creative imagination of our students. But we must never lose our grasp on the essential thing, that is to say the motors of play which arise from the natural dynamics of human relations and which audiences recognise immediately. The dynamics I refer to are the shared references which are indispensable for both actors and spectators. They are at work in all forms of theatre, including the most abstract. Reality can also be found in abstraction! We need to continually check these dynamic laws of theatre. That is why the second year is largely oriented towards writing, in the sense of the structuring of play. An actor can only truly play when the driving structure of the written play allows him to do so.

We do not deal with the symbolic dimensions of drama, as exemplified in Asian theatre traditions. Such traditions demonstrate symbolic theatre that has crystallised into its perfect form. When matter becomes saturated, it crystallises into a geometric form which is fixed and immutable. This quality characterises the Japanese Noh and the Kathakali. They have reached perfection in forms which are ideal for what they aim to achieve. Although the actors in these traditions must, of course, inhabit these forms, and nourish them, they do not have to invent them. I prefer to work on theatres whose forms are still open to change and renewal.

Three sets of questions guide our geodramatic exploration:

(1) What are the stakes that are being played for? What part of human nature is brought into play in melodrama, *commedia dell'arte*, tragedy? What elements of human behaviour and which bodies do they set in motion? What are the dramatic motors driving these forms of theatre?
(2) Which are the most appropriate stage idioms or languages for expressing these stakes? Half-masks, real objects, chorus? How do these languages work and how may they be combined?

(3) Which plays to choose? Which dramatic texts can best
enrich the exploration of each of the territories?

The second year is based on these three questions, supported by a
simple demand that all the students 'tell us a story'.

1

Gestural Languages

From pantomime to cartoon mime

Before beginning to explore dramatic territory, we begin the second year by working on gestural languages, taking physical expression in the different directions set out below. The purpose of this approach is to enrich all the students' subsequent investigations by providing them with a shared vocabulary in the languages of gesture.

In pantomime, gestures replace words. Where speech uses a word, a gesture must be found to signify it in pantomime. The origins of this language are partly in fairground theatre, where performers had to make themselves understood in a very noisy environment, but mostly in the ban on speaking that was served on the Italian actors, to prevent them from competing with the Comédie Française.[22] Pantomime was born from a constraint similar to that found in prisons, where convicts communicate by gesture, or in the Stock Exchange today. Its technique, which is partly traditional – one need only think of Deburau[23] – is a dead end for the theatre, and the only escape is through virtuosity. It requires an ability to draw objects and images in space, to come up with symbolic attitudes (some of which are found in oriental theatre).

Pantomime which restricts itself to a gestural translation of words is what I call white pantomime – a term borrowed from the period when Pierrot was a central character. Its technique relies mainly on hand gestures, supported by the attitude of the body. Inevitably, it requires a special syntax which is different from that of spoken language. 'You are pretty, come with me, let's go swimming' becomes: 'You and me ... you pretty ... go together ... swim ... over there.' A different logic is needed for the construction of phrases, which demands clarity, economy and precision of meaning.

Students often try to repeat gestures from everyday life which are borrowed from the language of pantomime. In fact, pantomime requires highly developed gestures which go beyond the everyday and establish a different rhythm from that of spoken language. Another pitfall is to replace every single word with a grimace. We have to recover a use of the face as 'mobile mask', one which can change expression in the course of a sentence, according to the feelings expressed, but not word by word.

Figurative mime, the second language we study, consists of using the body to represent not words but objects, architecture, furnishings. Two main possibilities are open to the actor: either to use his body to play a door, which another actor will open and close (the body of one thus becoming the stage set for the other), or the actor creates in space the virtual reality of a house – the roof, the walls, the windows, the door – so that it takes shape for the spectators, and so that the character can then go in and out. Although it has its limits, this language facilitates a technical approach to the articulation of gesture and will prove fruitful later on.

Cartoon mime, a language which is close to silent cinema, uses gesture to release the dynamic force contained within images. Rather than the actor representing words or objects on his own, this language is made up of images expressed collectively. Let us imagine a character going down into a cellar by the light of a candle. The actors can represent both the flame and the smoke, the shadows on the walls and the steps of the staircase. All these images can be suggested by the actors' movements, in silent play. One of the first exercises consists of building sequences of images; for example, the sequence we created one day, based on a visit to Mont-Saint-Michel.

The students began by suggesting the Mont-Saint-Michel seen from the distance, using their hands, then their bodies, alone or in small groups. Then, gradually, they took us into the picture. The place grew before our eyes, we moved onto the causeway, leaving the sea on both sides. We entered the gateway of the fortified city, going along the narrow street. We reached the restaurant of La Mère Poulard, then, through their images, we entered the restaurant, landed up in a plate, inside an omelette, and finished, along with the omelette, absorbed into the body of the diner.

This kind of continuous travelling shot requires the use of a widely varied gestural repertoire. It is worth noting that computer-generated images of virtual reality operate according to the same mechanism.

In their *auto-cours* I ask a group of students to recreate a whole film without words, using only gestures. Cartoon mime can make use of any cinematic technique: close-ups, long-shots, illusions, flashbacks, in short the whole repertoire of the modern language of moving pictures, with its rhythms, its brilliance, its ellipses, all transposed into the dimensions of theatre.

A deeper stratum of this research led us to explore the hidden gestures, emotions, underlying states of a character, which we express through *mimages*. These are a kind of 'close-up' on the character's internal dramatic state. Feelings are never performed or explained, but the actor produces lightning gestures which express, through a different logic, the character's state at a given moment (a sort of physical aside commenting on one phase of the performance).

A person has to go and see his boss to ask him for something. He arrives in front of the door, and is filled with a sense of anxiety: 'What shall I say to him?' At this precise moment, gestures provide an image of his feeling. Not explanatory gestures describing his state, but much more abstract movements which allow him to exteriorise elements which are naturally hidden in everyday behaviour. He knocks on the door, enters, he is afraid. Here again, the actor does not play fear by trembling or stammering; the fear within him is given gestural form, either by him alone or by another actor, or several. These lightning gestures demonstrate to the spectators an 'echo' of the character's fear which, of course, the other protagonists cannot see.

Storyteller mimes apply these different languages to the telling of stories. The idea is to tell a story by alternating between (sometimes by combining) the different gestural languages and the tale being told. This can be done solo, where the same actor is both storyteller and mime, or in a group, where a storyteller works with several mimes. We explore this relationship in all its dimensions, from the most intimate (the storyteller mime who sits at a table and performs with his hands) to the exploitation of the largest space (storyteller mimes performing on stage to the accompaniment of musicians, a chorus, a hero, etc.). This work is part of the great tradition of storytelling which exists in many countries, in China or in Africa, where the telling of a tale is accompanied by the gestural evocation of images.

Through all these ideas, students discover the different forms of the languages of mime: the language of situation (I am sitting, reading a book, there is a scratch at the door, I turn round, another scratch, I am frightened. The door opens ... a cat comes in); the language of action (I am carrying a sack of potatoes, I hoist it onto my back, I deposit it in my car, I get into the car and drive off); the language of suggestion (I look out over Paris from Montmartre and evoke everything that I can see: the lightness of the air, the roofs of the apartment blocks, the Eiffel Tower. I bring these images into being outside myself, impressionistically); the 'profound' *mimage* (finding gestures to express whatever has no image in our interior space). These languages will be valuable throughout the year for the short performance exercises which go on in the school. Some students will retain these types of language in their future lives as performers.

As a teaching method, this kind of work at the beginning of the year involves the whole group in play that develops technique progressively. It is a sort of warm-up before we plunge into the dramatic territories to come. It is important not to see the technical dimension of the different languages as an end in itself, but to enrich it continuously with dramatic states. It's no use being able to play a sun if the solar dynamic is missing from your gesture. It's no use being able to suggest the moon, if paleness fails to appear in the rhythm of your movement.

2

The Main Dramatic Territories

Melodrama

Grand emotions

Melodrama made its first appearance at the school in 1974 in response to a question which preoccupied me greatly at the time: 'Why is it that when a person says something he believes in, some people will accept what is said, while others will make fun of it?' Faced with this question, I decided to explore two possible forms of response. One was to believe in absolute values: in love, in family, in honour. I asked the actors to fight as hard as they could to compel their audience to accept these convictions. This produced melodrama. The other response was to make fun of everything: of God, of the Vietnam war, of AIDS. That produced *bouffons*.

In melodrama all the grand emotions come into play: good and evil, morality with innocence, sacrifice, treason, etc. The objective is to achieve a performance which is powerful enough to move spectators to tears by giving vent to these grand emotions. We aim to produce real tears. Now this can only be achieved if the characters really do believe in absolute values, and with such conviction that they are ready to sacrifice themselves. It becomes a matter of good against evil, courage against cowardice, purity against corruption. With time, the students have become more and more attached to this melodramatic territory and to its themes of morality and justice.

In melodrama, regrets, remorse, vindictiveness, shame, vengeance all come into play. Time is always a factor, hence the two principal themes essential to the territory of melodrama: 'The Return' and

'The Departure'. We begin working on 'The Soldier's Return', a theme with ancient roots in popular theatre.

After many years away at the wars, on a snowy winter's night, a soldier returns to his lonely house on the plain. He knocks at the door. It is opened. By the fire he finds his wife, two children and a new husband. She thought he was dead but she recognises him. He too recognises her, but neither shows it. He asks if he can stay the night. He is received, comforted, warmed. In the course of improvised scenes, in which he is left alone with the different characters, we discover that one of the children is his, the other is not. In the end, since the wife appears happy, the soldier sets off once more.

Working on this scenario, two elements are particularly important for the teacher. One is the subtlety of the actors' strategic play, which is responsible for bringing out surprise, rhythm, different reactions. Everything has to be played out through exchange of looks and silences, in a very moving manner. Who will open the door? How will the soldier and his wife recognise one another? How should the discovery be timed and the surprise be registered? In order to construct the situation, the students have to demonstrate a special mastery of timing. Secondly, I am very attentive to the way the actors play the scene. I ask them to believe completely in what they are performing, so that the public will share this belief. They must never over-emphasise nor use melodramatic clichés, but play out a timeless situation, as found in the plays of Ruzzante, or Brecht.

To take this research deeper, the theme is subdivided into: the knock at the door and reactions to it; the entry of the soldier and recognition by the wife, etc. Each sequence is analysed with precision, students passing the roles on from one to another for the different phases of the improvisation.

'The Departure for America', which is the next subject I suggest, raises the great theme of exile. A Sicilian left home carrying an old suitcase tied up with string and, after heart-rending farewells at the port of Palermo, went off to make his fortune in America. (In the

United States there are towns named Fortuna or Eureka after the cries uttered by the exiles when they arrived!) We can see this theme in the most up-to-date of situations. For example, the African worker leaving his village to come to France so as to earn enough to feed the family he has left behind. The students have a free choice of situation through which to explore this multi-track theme. They can also deal with 'The Departure' itself, 'Arrival in the New Place', 'Difficulties Encountered', 'The Family Back Home', 'The Arrival of a Letter'. They can move from one to the other, in counterpoint or in parallel, however they choose. With these melodramatic themes we come close to the tragedy of ordinary people, the drama of the everyday human struggle to survive, very different from what we shall find in great tragedy, where they have to struggle with the gods.

One of the main difficulties for students is the fear of getting right inside such grand emotions in front of spectators who will sometimes laugh at them. To perform melodrama, the actor must compel the audience to share his convictions. He can never harbour doubts about what he will say. Whatever is true for him will also be true for his audience. It is vital that the students be trained to accept this dimension. Although they must, of course, be prepared to perform parody when the author calls for it (Alfred Jarry, for example), they must never settle for a performance style which is itself parodic.

Lastly, they must also avoid the traps set by clichés. To speak of melodrama does not mean referring to a style of acting, but rather discovering and throwing light on very specific aspects of human nature. Melodrama is not outdated, it is of today and is all around us, in the man waiting for the telephone to ring to hear if he has a job, in the war-torn family, in the migrant worker, etc.

To enrich this territory, we make use of dramatic texts which relate to it. For example, a scene from *The Cherry Orchard* by Chekhov.

This passage demonstrates the dynamics of farewell which we studied with the neutral mask. In this scene the characters are leaving the house in which they have lived, some with regret, others with hope. In order to explore the diversity of possible interpretations, we study the different ways of doing it: laughingly; without turning round; making a break with the past; with a nostalgic gaze at the house; etc.

> RANYEVSKAYA. Another ten minutes, and we'll get into the carriages . . . (*Glances round the room.*) Farewell, dear house. Farewell, old grandfather house. The winter will go by, spring will come, and then soon you won't be here – they'll be pulling you down. So many things these walls have seen! (*Fervently kisses her daughter.*) My treasure, you're radiant, your eyes are sparkling like two diamonds. You're pleased, then? Very pleased?
> ANYA. Very pleased. There's a new life beginning, Mama!
>
> Anton Chekhov, *The Cherry Orchard*, in *Plays* (*trans. Michael Frayn*), London: Methuen, 1988, p. 341

The type of performance language which relates most closely to the melodramatic territory is that of cartoon mime. It is a form of expression universally recognised today, which accentuates the necessary shortcuts and uses instantaneous 'flashes', made up of startling images in which time and space are foreshortened. It thus brings together melodramatic imagery – orphans abandoned on the church steps – and the modern cinematic forms. I call it melomime.

Commedia dell'arte

The human comedy

The *commedia dell'arte* and its masks were part of my teaching at the school from the very beginning. Sadly, over the course of time, a so-called 'Italian' style of performance, which is nothing but clichés, has begun to spread. Young actors have often done short courses in *commedia* and the playing has become lifeless. The very name *commedia* began to irk me. For these reasons I have been led to turn the problem inside out, to discover what lies beneath, that is to say *la comédie humaine* (the human comedy). From this point on, using a much broader field of reference, we have rediscovered our creative freedom.

This territory brings into play all the great trickeries of human nature: persuading people, duping them, taking advantage: it deals in urgent desires and its characters are concerned with survival. In the *commedia dell'arte* everyone is credulous and cunning; hunger, love, money are the motivating forces. The fundamental theme is how to lay a trap for whatever reason: to get the girl, the money, food and drink. The characters are rapidly betrayed by their own stupidity and find themselves ensnared in their own plots. Pushed to its extreme, this pattern characterises *la comédie humaine*, bringing to the surface the tragedy that lies buried beneath it. Very different from his chirpy cliché, Harlequin really tries to understand what is happening to him, though he fails. This is when the limits of human nature emerge: why aren't we cleverer, why can't we understand? All the characters are frightened: frightened of being tricked, of starving, of dying, etc. It is this deep-seated fear which gives rise to Pantalone's avarice: he is holding on! This tragic depth is an essential element exploited by Molière in his plays.

I first ask the students to construct their own half-masks. The first assignment requires them to make a half-mask for a character they would like to play, with no reference whatever to the *commedia dell'arte*. Starting with a very simple mask, they gradually add a nose, colour, a moustache, etc. Together we explore the range of these masks in performance, their characteristics and the links that can be established between them. Only after this do I introduce the traditional masks of the *commedia dell'arte*: Harlequin and Pantalone, but also Brighella, the Captain, the Doctor, Tartaglia, etc.

Two main characters have survived from the tradition: Harlequin

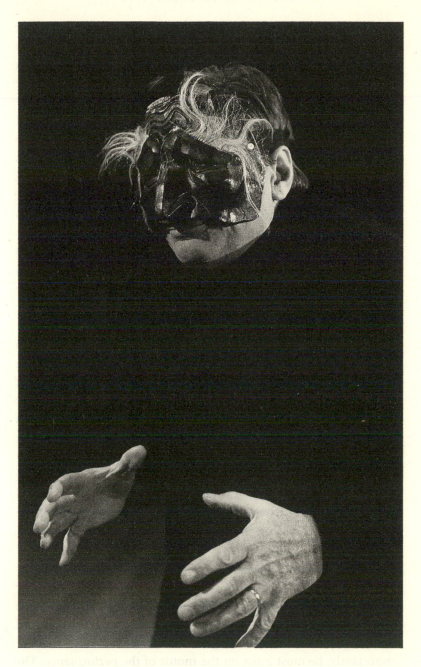

Jaques Lecoq wearing the mask of Pantalone

the servant and Pantalone his master. Harlequin, originally one of the *zanni* characters, a credulous, cunning peasant from the Bergamo area, has become a mischievous, clever schemer. In Molière, following a two-hundred-year evolution, this character became Scapin. Pantalone, merchant of Venice, M.D., trader in treasures from the Middle East, is highly intelligent. He is robbed under the spell of love, naively believing that he is always loved by beautiful girls. Hence the pity which we may feel for him. This tragic undercurrent in the comedy can arouse laughter in the spectators, never in the characters themselves.

It is necessary to work from scenarios, a method which has been refined over the years with the help of audiences. Although this way of working has been handed down by tradition from father to son, we have to prevent it becoming mechanical by returning again and again to situations which allow the complex humanity of the characters to emerge.

Commedia dell'arte is an art of childhood. It moves swiftly from one situation to another and from one state to the next. Harlequin is capable of passing in an instant from tears at the death of Pantalone to delight that his soup is ready. This means that the *commedia* is a cruel territory, but also one which offers fabulous opportunities for play. The themes we use are very simple: 'Harlequin scratches himself' or 'Harlequin eats spaghetti', 'Pantalone counts his money'. 'Someone calls for someone' can become a major theme, provided, of course, that the person who is called for never comes! Between the call of one and the arrival of the other there is room for all the theatre in the world.

Not all these themes can be improvised. Some demand preparation, which the students work on in their *auto-cours*. The teacher must keep his eye on two complementary elements: on the one hand the scenario, the story, the points which have to be covered by the players when they improvise; on the other, and more importantly, he must insist on the motor of the performance. The driving force is not *what* to play but *how* it should be played. What forces are brought into play? Who is pulling? Who is pushing? Who is pulling or pushing himself? Who is being pulled or pushed? By answering these simple questions, we can give the sequence its dynamic. While a scenario is linear, proceeding from one point to another, the driving force is dynamic, introducing the ups and downs necessary for performance, and this dynamic can never remain horizontal. Moreover, in the *commedia dell'arte*, it breaks free from the limits of everyday behaviour, reaching an imaginary dimension. You don't smile, you die laughing!

In the *commedia dell'arte/comédie humaine*, the performance style is pushed to the limit and situations are taken to their extreme point. The performer achieves a very high level of acting and the spectators have the chance to see particular behaviour taken to its logical conclusion in death, even though it turns out to be feigned.

> *Pantalone is at home, counting his money. A servant comes to say that someone wants to see him. He asks who it is. The servant doesn't know. 'Is he tall?' Yes. 'Is he old?' Yes. 'Does he walk like this?' Yes. Now he knows: it's his friend Brigante, who made him a loan, and has come to ask for his money back. 'I won't see him,' he says. Too late, Brigante has already entered. They embrace . . . 'Dear friend, what a pleasure to see you . . .' They play the comedy of friendship. After which come the lazzi. A chair is brought: 'What a fine chair!' says Brigante, who is already working out its price. 'It's a very old one,' replies Pantalone . . .*

Here the motor driving the play is 'appreciate/depreciate'. Pantalone will attempt to play down the value of everything he has, while Brigante will try to estimate the worth of the things he anticipates may come to him. Next Brigante will try to discuss the matter which brings him to Pantalone's house: the repayment of the debt, while Pantalone will avoid the subject, talk of other things, change the subject. Here the driving force becomes deviation, up until the fateful moment when Brigante will manage to say: 'Give me back my money.' And Pantalone will drop dead from a heart attack! Only to revive, of course, as soon as Brigante has gone off to fetch the doctor, for death here is just another ploy.

To perform this type of theme the students can wear either the traditional masks, or the ones which they have made themselves, but I have noticed that they are freer to adapt the principles of this kind of playing when they are wearing their own masks. As soon as Harlequin or Pantalone is mentioned, their idea of the tradition intervenes and weighs them down.

Scenarios and strategic play

The first thing I look for is the students' ability to develop a strategic sense in their playing. How do they succeed in developing or unravelling a situation? How do they manage a reversal of situation (e.g. 'The Robber Robbed')? How do they handle a rhythmical exchange of words? The Italian language is better suited to this than French, because it is more percussive, less fluid.

One of the difficulties encountered with the half-mask concerns the voice. In the first year, the students had seldom been asked to speak, and now they are faced with enormous freedom in the use of words. So they tend to use their own voice, which is not possible while wearing the mask. They have to work to find the character's voice, a public voice that has the measure of masked performance. Just as you cannot move as you do in real life when wearing a mask, so you cannot speak a part in a half-mask without honing it to its essentials. In a half-mask, the text itself is masked. Psychological performance becomes impossible. The dialogue tends towards the *botta e risposta* [statement and reply], which the lovers perform unmasked.

The characters of the Italian comedy are constantly oscillating between two contradictory poles. Harlequin is, at one and the same time, naive and cunning, the Captain is strong and scared, the Doctor knows everything and understands nothing, Pantalone is both an industrial boss, master of himself and helplessly off his head when in love. This duality, pushed to its limit, is a source of great richness.

In the *commedia dell'arte* you die of everything: of desire, of hunger, of love, of jealousy. In this sense this dramatic territory is an extension of what ordinary life can bring. That is why the level of playing will be pushed to the limit, to acrobatics. However, it is impossible to remain permanently in a state of emotional extremity – you cannot die or starve all the time – and so the characters are always thrown brutally back and forth from one feeling to another. Laughter, when pushed over the edge, turns to tears, and we see that the gestures are the same for both. Whether he is laughing or crying, Harlequin rolls around on the ground in the same way!

Lazzi provide the basic opportunity for playfulness in the *commedia dell'arte*. In the books of *commedia* scenarios the most interesting points are those where nothing is spelled out and the one word *lazzi* is written. This part of the text can only be brought to life by the actor, through his performance and his comic presence. The apparent thinness of the scenarios is due to the difficulty of writing down on paper what you must do if you are to be funny, touching, convincing. The performer is the missing element. The great difference between gags and *lazzi* is that the latter always have a human reference. A gag can be purely mechanical or absurd; it can leave one kind of logic behind and suggest a different one, but the *lazzo* always brings out an element of the character's humanity.

> *Harlequin and Brighella have been ordered to prepare a meal for some guests. They lay the table and begin to point out where each of the guests will sit, then they go through the whole menu, dish by dish, in their imaginations. They move from the small delights of the starters to gross guzzling and end up completely stuffed. In this way they imagine a whole gigantic feast in which, of course, they will have no share.*

Although the *commedia dell'arte* is based on real situations, objects can also be brought into play in fantastic ways. Harlequin's stick may serve him as a tail, may replace his hand when he wants to

WOMAN Reason...
MAN Duty...
WOMAN Saved her.
MAN Freed him.
WOMAN Barbarian!
MAN Wretch!
WOMAN What did you say?
MAN What did you mutter?
WOMAN I say I hate you.
MAN I say I detest you.
WOMAN I can't bear the sight of you.
MAN I can no longer put up with you.
WOMAN You reject those ties...
MAN You reject those chains...
WOMAN Which you said were golden.
MAN Which you said were made of diamonds.
WOMAN They turned out to be false.
MAN They turned out to be glass.
WOMAN Gilded iron!
MAN Mock diamonds!
WOMAN That's why I tore them off.
MAN That's why I broke them.
WOMAN Now I rejoice.
MAN Now I am free.
WOMAN Go on then, break those ties!
MAN Go on then, destroy those chains!
WOMAN I am free!
MAN I am independent!
WOMAN No more slavery!
MAN No more obstacles!
WOMAN The knot is undone.
MAN The ties are broken.

Constant Mic, 'Scorn against scorn' in *La Commedia dell'Arte*, Paris: Pléiade, 1927 (trans. D.B.)

shake hands without touching. Pantalone's purse may hang between his legs. Objects here are not just props, they facilitate the development of rich fantasy. That is why we never mime objects; we make genuine use of them.

Very few genuine *commedia* texts survive, with the exception of the scenarios and the *botta e risposta*. Because of this we also explore the playwrights who made use of this territory: Molière, Ruzzante, Gozzi, Goldoni, but also Shakespeare and Goethe. It is impressive to see how many authors were influenced in their poetic works by the Italian players who travelled across Europe. For teaching purposes, my preference is for the beginnings of *commedia*, the plays of Ruzzante. Also early Molière, his early farces rather than his more psychological *Don Juan* or *The Misanthrope*.

Too often the *commedia dell'arte* is associated with the notion of improvisation. But in fact it was not improvised at all. Although variations were sometimes introduced, the performances were passed down from father to son in a highly structured fashion. The Italian actors had a repertoire of situations and *lazzi* which they inserted at the right moments. When the Piccolo Teatro were in Paris performing Goldoni's *Harlequin, Servant of Two Masters*, Giorgio Strehler, who directed it, insisted on respecting strictly what was written in the text. One day, when he was not watching the performance, the actors added twenty minutes onto the show's running time. The director was furious when he discovered this self-indulgence.

The physical technique we use is the same as that of all masked theatres in the world. For the body to be able to communicate with the public in this form of theatre, as we have said, it needs to be perfectly articulated. I have therefore put together a gymnastic routine for Harlequin. The acrobatic dimension is of course present, with its dramatic justification, as always. When Pantalone falls into a rage and does a somersault, the spectators should not say: 'What a wonderful somersault!', but 'What an amazing rage!' To achieve this level of physical commitment and to justify this gesture, an extraordinary emotive charge is required, as well as perfect technique in the somersault.

Shouts, gesticulations and unnecessarily exaggerated performances are the most frequent signs of actors' inability to hit the mark. When the students are not good enough to reach the required acting level, they try in vain to compensate by shouting. For this reason the *commedia* is very difficult for young actors. At twenty, the students have not lived enough; in particular they lack the tragic dimension which is an important aspect of this territory. Despite this, we continue with this work at the school, not for immediate use, but so that students will retain a memory, both physical and mental, of this level of acting, and will be able to use it later.

Theatre people have often dreamed of recreating a contemporary *commedia dell'arte*, hoping to renew the archetypes by inserting them into contemporary society or politics. This has always seemed to me to be a dubious undertaking because, historically, the social relations of the *commedia* are immutable. There are masters and there are servants, but the idea is not to change society. It is to shed light on human nature through its comedy, made up of the deceptions and compromises which are indispensable to the survival of the characters. Harlequin does not go on strike: he comes to an arrangement. Pantalone never goes bankrupt, despite his claims. The *commedia* belongs to every time and every place as long as there are masters and servants which are essential to it. These timeless elements of the human comedy interest me for the way they can enable the students, who are of course 'contemporary', to invent a new theatre of their own time.

Bouffons

Mystery, the grotesque and the fantastic

In the years since they emerged in response to my question about 'people who believe in nothing and make fun of everything', the *bouffons* have evolved quite a bit. Many variations have developed, opening the way to a vast territory which we needed to explore. The first stage was through parody. It consisted simply of making fun of another person by means of mimicry. Take anyone in the street: merely by imitating their way of walking you can mock and parody them. The same goes for the voice and general behaviour. Mimicry was thus the first, relatively friendly stage in the exploration of '*bouffonesque*' mockery.

The second stage was to make fun, not only of what the person did, but also of his deepest convictions. For example, I would ask someone to make a reasoned speech in public, a scientific or mathematical lecture, for example, and meanwhile another student was told to make the public laugh by imitating the lecturer. In the process, I noticed that it becomes quite unbearable seeing someone dressed in a suit making fun of someone dressed the same way: it rapidly turned very spiteful and so difficult to handle that I decided that the person making fun had necessarily to be distinct from his victim. He had to be different.

For this reason, I tried to construct a different body, a *bouffonesque* body, puffed up, obese. I asked the students to alter their shape by adding false buttocks and bellies. Out of this emerged some interesting shapes: thin young women, who had felt ill-at-ease with their bodies, would bring huge anatomies to life, figures with bulging breasts and fleshy buttocks. Working in the opposite direction, other students would emerge with stringy, rangy physiques. By means of this corporeal transformation, in these artificial, reinvented bodies, they suddenly felt freer. They dared to do things which they would never have achieved with their own bodies. In this way, their whole physique became a mask. Confronted with these *bouffonesque* bodies, the characters being parodied were more willing to be made fun of by these fools; it became less of an issue, and there was no conflict between the *bouffon* and the object of his mockery. We were finding our way back to the tradition of the king's fool, who, far from being a real madman, was licensed to express truth in all its forms. In a *bouffonesque* body, the person who mocks can say the unsayable, going so far as to mock what 'cannot' be mocked: war, famine, God. It was through the *bouffons* that we got to know about AIDS before there was a widespread awareness of this illness. By performing a procession on the theme 'The Death of Love' in a *bouffonesque* transposition, they were able to make us accept the unacceptable.

I noticed that the people who laughed at everything, even the most sacred values, created a space for the mystery of things. They touched on the great territory of tragedy. Their mockery turned to tragedy, in much the same way that the violence of Steven Berkoff's[24] writing achieves beauty. For me this was a great discovery. So I went on to wonder where these *bouffons* came from. They could not derive from a realist space like the street or the metro. They must have their origin elsewhere: in mystery, the night, heaven and earth. Their function was not to make fun of a particular individual, but more generally of everyone, of society as a whole. *Bouffons* enjoy themselves, for their whole life is spent having fun imitating aspects of human life. Their great delight is to make war, fight, tear out each other's guts. However, their war games never follow the logical chronology of a story that unfolds. They bring a special style of composition: they so enjoy killing one another that with each killing they want to start again. So they indulge in repeated mutual massacres just for the fun of it.

This was where short cuts came in, bringing ellipses which are a specific part of the *bouffons'* play: someone who had been wounded was rushed to hospital. In the logic of the *bouffons*, for the hospitals to function, there had to be lots of people dying, and to supply this need people had to keep on killing one another. For there to be people killing one another, there had to be war, and so it built up. This type of situation brings out the absurdity in the way human life is organised. *Bouffons* deal essentially with the social dimension of human relations, showing up its absurdities. They also deal with hierarchies of power, and their reversal. Every *bouffon* has someone above him and someone beneath; he looks up to one and is looked up to by the other. Only the person at the lowest level of this hierarchy has no one to look up to him. He's the one who scribbles graffiti in the toilets, his sole meagre means of expression. The most powerful *bouffon* – prince, director, president or king – will decide on a whim that the war has gone on long enough in one place and it is time it started up somewhere else. So all the others follow. In fact, *bouffons* operate on the basis of the reversal of power: the one in charge is the most feeble-minded.

After looking at *bouffons* on their own, we tried to work out how they could get together, and we discovered that they live in gangs. The ideal gang is formed by a group of five *bouffons*, who can establish a strong degree of complicity. Beyond this number, they begin to turn into a chorus, a subject which we shall come back to later. A gang of *bouffons* has a boss. The whole gang has to help him work out what he wants to say. We saw gangs of little *bouffons* approaching us with the enormous head of a prophet; he had no body but he had come to unveil a mystery, before collapsing. We also found that these gangs often include an innocent, who wanders about among the others without ever disturbing the order of things. He is a strange figure, a necessary mistake!

In the course of time, a number of major families of *bouffons* have emerged: the mystery group, the power group and finally a gang even madder than the rest, the science group. These three families have led us to settle, today, on three distinct, almost separate territories, which are mystery, the grotesque and the fantastic.

Mystery borders on quasi-religious belief. The *bouffons* from this family are soothsayers. They know the future. They know the end of the world and can foretell it. They know the mysteries of the times before birth and after death. They are prophets.

The bouffons *of mystery emerge from the night in a procession; they dance to the beat of percussion, warming up the playing space. They bring The Word with them, but it is sleeping. Then the little devils*

The *bouffons* of mystery

arouse their prophet, who rises up, enlightened, to describe the end of
the world. The bouffons *mime images of the Apocalypse and have fun*
parodying them. Having seen into the future, The Word collapses. It is
carried away into the night to the sound of drums. On this occasion
texts of great mystery and beauty are spoken by the devil's bouffons.

They speak like Job questioning Heaven, or like Dante in *The
Divine Comedy*. The English *bouffons* inhabit Shakespearean
country. We have given *bouffons* the greatest texts and the greatest
poets to recite. Who better than a *bouffon* to recite a text by
Antonin Artaud? Paradoxically, it can be better understood in this
form than at a so-called poetry reading. Poets are the greatest
fools.

The grotesques are close to caricature. They have the same
relationship to everyday life that can be seen in humorous
drawings. They never deal with feelings or with psychology, but
only with social functions. Daumier's[25] set of prints depicting the
different professions have this dimension. In the dramatic repertoire, a character like Jarry's Ubu belongs to this world.

The fantastics are especially present today. They make use of
electronics and of science, but also draw on the wildest flights of
fantasy. We have seen people with several heads, animal-human
combinations, *bouffons* whose head was in their belly. Every
madness is possible here: it constitutes the freedom and the beauty
of the actor.

The term *bouffon* can thus be seen to cover an extremely large
territory, whose borders cannot be fixed. This is why I ask the
students to explore as much of the ground as possible, so that they
will have some experience of each of the three major pathways.
Because of this, they cannot stay with the first image they find, but
have to get involved in a genuinely creative process. It is important
to point out that a single *bouffon* cannot belong to all three
families, although some combinations are possible within the same
gang. The fantastic can exist alongside mystery or, again, a *bouffon*
of mystery may turn into a grotesque, passing from one state to
the other without our being sure which is which. A gang of

Oh grant us heads of burning coals
Skulls scorched by bolts from heaven
Lucid heads, real heads
Shot through with your presence

May we be born to inward skies
Riddled with tumbling abysses
And may we be pierced by vertigo.
With an incandescent claw

Satiate our hunger
For inter-stellar turmoil
Ah fill us with astral lava
Instead of our blood

Tear us loose. Split us
With your hands of cutting coals
Open to us those burning roads
Where we die on the far side of death

Make our brains reel
At the centre of their so-called science
Implant in us a new intelligence
With claws that tear like typhoons.

Antonin Artaud, 'Prière' from *Tric-Trac du ciel* in *Oeuvres
complètes*, vol. 1, Paris: Gallimard, 1970 (trans. D.B.)

fantastic *bouffons* appears on stage; suddenly it metamorphoses into a gang of little grotesques. This can be a disturbing situation for the public, losing touch with a logical system and moving into a different dimension.

A different body

The specific language of *bouffons* emerged with our research into the gestures and actions which might make up this different body. Some approached the human body in the spirit of the Michelin Man, a sort of outsize human ball, while others distanced themselves from it. One of my great discoveries was the extent to which the international dimension of the school came out in the different *bouffonesque* images nurtured by each culture. The South Americans expressed their imaginative fantasies through their flying animals and their animal-human combinations. The French went back to the Rabelaisian tribe of jovial cooks. English *bouffons* are close to Hogarth's figures. The Spanish experience the tragedy of the fiesta. The Italians bring song and dance and music. The Northerners are more mysterious, halfway between day and night in the madness of twilight. Germany contributed her great mythological fantasies. The Asians brought dragons and devils to life. This dramatic territory is the one which, more than any other, underlines the deep cultural differences between students.

From the pedagogic point of view, the *bouffons'* territory is particularly difficult to handle, especially since we are constantly researching new creative processes. So the students have to be set in motion so that they can discover for themselves the elements which I have mentioned or even invent new ones.

I begin, as always, with the body. The first step is very simple: I ask each of them to draw a *bouffon* on a sheet of paper. At this stage in the work the students have no conception of what we are embarking on, nor of the nature of the territory. Each draws his *bouffon*, according to his own idea, and then I give my comments on these drawings. I pick out those who have a 'cultural' vision – the ones who draw little bells on hats, harking back to carnival ideas – or those who suggest madness – drawings of people who are unkempt and shaggy. These drawings are kept, but not used. I give them back to the students at the end of the course without making any comment, as something that can give them food for thought in private.

Next they must create their *bouffon* physically. We provide cloth, foam rubber, clothes, objects, ribbon, string and each student is free to create his *bouffon*'s body. Then we work together on the kinds of movements they make. The ones with fleshy buttocks have fun making them wobble, others play with their long tails, or scratch themselves with their outsize fingernails. In this phase of the work I insist that the costumes are never seen as finished and are never too elaborate. They must remain provisional, relatively rudimentary, dispensable, open to development in the course of research before their ultimate conclusion, at the end of the course, in a more finalised form.

No one is more of a child than the *bouffon* and no one is more of a *bouffon* than a child. This is why, in parallel with the work on the body, we do preparatory improvisations leading towards the *bouffonesque* dimension on the theme of 'Childhood'. We try to find our way back to childhood using different techniques.

The first theme is the town square, with children playing in the sandpit, at cops and robbers or at tag, etc. We try out a range of possible behaviours in this situation: playful, spiteful, gentle, aggressive, possessive, comic. We are not looking for an external performance of child-characters, nor for a reversion to childishness, but for a genuine rediscovery of the childhood state: its loneliness, its demands, its obsessions, its search for rules, these are all elements which we shall find at work in the *bouffonesque* dimension.

Next I suggest that the children play at being grown-ups. They can play at mummies and daddies, they can play at being aeroplanes, but they can also play at war, as Lebanese children used to, with wooden machine-guns. After this, I make the reverse suggestion: the grown-ups play like children. Frontier-guards, on either side of a piece of wire laid on the ground, play at standing on it, displacing it, pushing it back, etc. We rapidly discover how much this game shows up our desire for possession and power over the 'other'.

In their rituals, *bouffons* do not invoke heavenly powers, they spit on them! They invoke earthy forces; they are on the side of the devil and the underworld. Emerging from the ground, they adopt human form. They invent rites which are theirs alone and which are completely incomprehensible to us, the uninitiated. They carry out strange processions, special ceremonies, parades with drums. A gang of *bouffons* will begin tapping their feet, dancing and singing, chanting wild fantasies, and all in a very organised, ritual manner. In these cases the actors themselves sometimes don't know what they are doing, but they do it! These rituals never give rise to conflict for there is no rivalry between *bouffons*. They never get angry with one another. Each has his place in a hierarchy which is highly organised but accepted by all. There are those who deal out beatings and those who are on the receiving end. And that's fine. Those on the receiving end ask for more: they like it. Each one has his accepted place in the society of *bouffons* which, for them, is the ideal society. Of course this society is ours too.

When *bouffons* appear on stage, it is always to depict society. Hence any theme is possible: war, television, the council of ministers or any other event taken from the news, which becomes an endless source of inspiration and for devising games. Sometimes they dress up like characters in society: they might put on an army cap, or a priest's cassock, and begin to play at being these characters. But they do it in their guise, constantly reverting to the original *bouffons* who always mock the characters they depict. If they decide to represent a trades union, they will never go into the psychology of this or that well-known personality, as a satirical television show might do – instead they will play at unionisation. They may set up a demonstration, moving alternately from being demonstrators to being policemen, just for the fun of it.

Work on *bouffons* draws on an instinct for play which can be adapted to different situations. Everything is in the way of doing it, in the treatment, the level of performance. The students devise their scripts according to a special logic. With any situation, *bouffons* will deform it, twist it, play it out in an unusual way. They might repeat the same word in a given text ten times over, coming back to it repeatedly, just for the pleasure of the repetition. They will turn any situation *buffonesque*. We are in the realm of organised madness.

As for the whole of the second year, this work involves exploring unknown territory. Whatever references there may be are brought in afterwards. Although I have sometimes felt that a performance reminded me of Hieronymus Bosch, or of a medieval mystery play, or of the carnival, I had no such references in mind at the outset. My knowledge of *bouffons* was gained through practical movement work, through improvisation, and not from books or from a tradition dictating any special technique. By their very nature, *bouffons* imposed a teaching method based on creativity.

At the conclusion of this exploration, many questions are still unanswered. Are *bouffons* self-sufficient? Can they construct a whole performance all by themselves? Or should they be seen in parallel with tragedy? Can they intervene in tragedy and how far can tragedy encroach on their territory? In order to find answers to these questions, I suggest an initial approach to *bouffons*, followed by work on tragedy, before trying all kinds of possible combinations. I retain the extraordinary memory of a gang of *bouffons* who, as if they were servants, brought a tragic chorus in on their shoulders, deposited them in front of the audience and then vanished. The chorus proceeded to speak a text from an Ancient Greek tragedy. It was a sublime vision.

134

Tragedy

Chorus and hero

Tragedy is the greatest dramatic territory of all, but also the greatest form of theatre that is still open to renewal. At the school we approach it by way of the discoveries I made while working on the chorus at Syracuse in Sicily, discoveries which I then applied to my teaching objectives. Far from taking an historical view of ancient tragedy and its imagined codes of communication, we seek to reinvent the tragic form for today.

The territory of tragedy raises the profoundest questions concerning our relationship to the gods, to destiny and to the transcendental. It has nothing to do with questions of sects or religions. Nowadays scientists are closest to these questions when they find themselves awed by the wonders of the cosmos. Scientific research engages with a territory which goes beyond the merely human and this is also true of tragedy, hence its link to the territory of the *bouffons*. Now that the gods have disappeared, the *bouffons* have moved in and replaced them. No doubt they too may disappear one day and make way for something else: for humanity to discover a new equilibrium, no longer torn between social and cosmic realities. It's up to the artists and scientists to continue this quest.

For the students, the major discovery when they work on tragedy is how to make connecting links. They discover what it really means to be connected, both with the ensemble and with a space. To speak through another's mouth, in a common choral voice, is to be, at one and the same time, grounded in the truth of a living character, and in touch with a dimension which transcends human reality. All of the actor's art is needed to establish a connecting link between these two apparently contradictory poles rather than being torn apart.

The shape of the territory of tragedy is marked by two main features: the chorus and the hero.

The tragic chorus

A chorus enters to the sound of percussion which gives a rhythm to the group. It fills the whole space, and then withdraws to one part of the stage. By so doing, it frees a new space and creates a kind of appeal to the hero. But who is able to fill this space? What balance can be found, today, between a chorus and a hero?

In order to introduce an understanding of chorus and hero, we conduct preliminary work on crowds and orators. The crowd is approached by means of improvisations. The subject of the first is Speaker's Corner at Hyde Park in London on a Sunday, when people get up on their soapboxes and try to attract the attention of the passers-by so as to lecture them.

We imagine a large square with lots of people walking about and we ask one student to attract their attention by any means in his power. When he manages this, he must go on to persuade them of the importance of his subject, and must put across a point of view which he believes in: for or against abortion, immigration, nuclear energy. What he is talking about matters less than his ability to hold his listeners' attention.

I insist that the students act, that is to say they must defend a point of view which they do not necessarily share. The distance this creates seems to me to be essential: it is better for the player to argue the case for the death penalty if he is personally against it, and vice versa. This improvisation can also bring a moment of truth for the actor himself: as soon as his public is bored they will wander off.

The next stage is to complete this exercise by bringing on a second character who contradicts the first by arguing the opposite case. Two groups begin to form, each listening to one of the orators: they are the forerunners of the chorus. Finally, I appoint a conductor, who is outside the game and who can direct the whole improvisation, putting some order into this great elemental chaos in which words fly back and forth between orators and crowds, and ensuring a basic rhythm for the game.

Tragedies cannot be improvised, they require authors. For our work on orators, we therefore abandon improvisation and turn to great texts from public life: the speeches of Angela Davis,[26] André Malraux's[27] oration for the transfer of Jean Moulin's[28] ashes to the Panthéon, or Charles de Gaulle's[29] cry of 'Vive le Québec libre!' in Montreal, Martin Luther King's speeches, etc. – in short, all the great speeches that have had the power to enthuse mass audiences. The actor who is to make the speech will reconstruct, with the help of other students, the place and the atmosphere in which it was originally delivered. He arranges the staging within the school and then performs it. This has provided us with some memorable moments: Hitler's speech to the SS one Christmas Eve, performed by a German actor in front of a crowd wearing swastika armbands, all standing to attention. That was a particularly painful replay. Another memory is 'Cataluña libre!', a speech for the independence of Catalonia delivered from the balcony of the school, with passers-by collecting together and making up the listening crowd.

Through these experiences, the students test out the emotional level which can unite a crowd, an orator and a text. The orator is the forerunner of the hero and the crowd suggests the humanity of the chorus. The transition from crowd to chorus involves raising the level of acting in the same way as the transition between psychological and masked performance. The tragic chorus is a crowd raised to the level of the mask.

Because the chorus always reacts to events or speeches, we do preparatory work on reaction chorus. A group of students is given the task of making clear to spectators what it is that they [i.e. the group] are watching, purely by means of their reactions to the event, for example a football match, a film, a bullfight.

In a box at the theatre, a group of spectators is watching a performance. The curtain rises, the lights come up and the show gets under way. We come to the big love scene between Romeo and Juliet. The spectators' reactions are all we need to make us imagine what is happening on stage: a greater level of attention as the curtain rises, a marked drawing together of two spectators as the lovers meet, a slight facial movement . . .

All these characters and situations must be conveyed to us by means of the reaction chorus. It is a difficult and a subtle procedure, for the students cannot simply watch what is going on, still less 'pantomime' it; instead they must find a language through which we can sense the dynamics and the emotion of what is taking place. Any means may be harnessed, including the language of analogy, which we call the double image. In this case an image appears which parallels another: someone drops a handkerchief on stage, and one of the spectators also drops his programme! What happens in the box is subtly analagous to the events taking place on stage.

The chorus is the one essential element in clearing a genuine space for tragedy. A chorus is not geometric but organic. In just the same way as a collective body, it has its centre of gravity, its extensions, its respiration. It is a kind of living cell, capable of taking on different forms according to the situation in which it finds itself. It may exhibit contradictions, its members may sometimes oppose one another in subgroups, or alternatively unite to address the public with one voice. I cannot imagine a tragedy without a chorus. But how are these people to be grouped? How can this collective body be brought to life? How can it be made to breathe and move like a living organism, avoiding both aestheticised choreography and militaristic geometry? The chorus is one of the most important components of my teaching method and, for those who have taken part in one, it is the most beautiful and the most moving dramatic experience.

The chorus is made up of a group of either seven or fifteen people. These figures are precise, for each number has its own specific dynamic. One person is solitude. Two is one and his double. Three make a unity, four a static block. A group of five begins to move, but each member retains a personality. Six is not worth considering, for it divides in half to make two threes. Seven is an interesting number: a chorus leader may emerge, flanked by two half-choruses of three each. Eight is a double block. At nine a crowd begins: a group of nine goes off in all directions. Ten and eleven are nearly a dozen! At thirteen the chorus starts to emerge. Fourteen is unworkable – there's always someone missing. Fifteen, as in rugby, is the ideal number: a chorus leader, two half-choruses of seven, each of which has a sub-leader, and all kinds of marvellous movements become possible. Above fifteen it becomes an invasion with inevitably military connotations. In order to work out and clarify these facts, I suggest a simple exercise:

A group of students walks about the room, filling the whole space. On a signal, they group themselves into twos, threes, fives, sevens, etc.

Together we watch how they come together, and then how each group can or cannot be made to move. Another type of exercise is when a chorus moves without anyone knowing who is the leader. The internal rule, which spectators are unaware of, but the students discover, is that the leader is inevitably the one visible to all the others. Or again, we make the chorus 'breathe' by maximising the distance between its members. Beyond a certain distance, the chorus no longer exists, it breaks up. Here we find the threshold of stress, known to architects.

In tragedy the role of the chorus is to warn, to give advice or sympathy; it is present throughout but never involves itself in the action. We have to remember that originally the Greek chorus was not on the same level as the actors. It had its own performance space and, through its reactions, it built a link between the public and the heroes. In Greek tragedy battles are never shown; the chorus simply reacts to accounts of them. The great rule governing the tragic chorus is never to be active, always reactive. In the end, the chorus always displays wisdom. The chorus is often thought of as composed of old men, but they are not necessarily ancient characters bent over their sticks, they may be sages, symbolic messengers bringing age-old wisdom to bear. To begin with the choruses are not mixed, and we work separately on men's and women's choruses. The finest choruses are often those made up of women, for they possess a deep sense of cohesion and solidarity. They stand guard over the essential values.

The dramatic movements of a chorus may be governed by feelings, but they may just as well take their impulse from the tragic movements seen in nature. Materials, especially, provide a tragic language which we can borrow. A sugar-lump which dissolves, a piece of paper which crumples, cardboard which folds, wood which splinters, cloth which rips, are all profoundly tragic movements. In the same way, it is interesting to dissolve a tragic chorus, to crumple it, to rip it apart. Through analogy, we are here reinvesting all the work we did in the first year on identification with materials.

There is always the risk of ending up with a militarised chorus, over-disciplined, clean and neat, in which everyone marches lifelessly together. Theatre directors often love this kind of work, not just so as to have a chorus in their productions, but as a point of reference for the spatial dimension involved in any group work. The chorus embodies ordered movement.

A balanced stage

The birth of the chorus begins with one of the finest exercises devised at the school: 'balancing the stage'. It consists of a game of balancing or unbalancing the stage by moving the actors around. Six benches, each two metres long, are arranged to form the shape of a rectangular stage. Ten more benches (two for each width and three for each length) surround this space; the participants take their places on them. The playing space must be rectangular and not circular, because a circle only allows for one kind of movement: turning. Or else it becomes a ritual space with a central fire around which everyone gathers. This explains why it is so difficult to perform in a theatre in the round. The circus ring is made for horses, not for people, who cannot establish a dynamic in it. A rectangle, on the other hand, allows for all the major dynamic movements: right angles, parallels, diagonals. These provide freedom and structure for a range of dramatic potentialities.

Let us imagine that this rectangular stage is balanced around a central axis. An actor who takes up a position alone, in the central zone, maintains the balance of the stage. If he moves outside this zone, he unbalances it and causes it to tilt. So a second actor is necessary to rebalance it by choosing a position in relation to the first actor. To start with, the players are spread all over the stage, and all are assumed to be of equal weight, despite physical differences. We shall not be seeking for storytelling performance on a realist stage, but to experience the sensations of fullness and emptiness, and these feelings will be shared by those on stage and those on the benches.

$1 = 1$

A first rule is the starting point. The stage is empty. 'A' gets up and positions himself in the centre (which is not the precise point where diagonals intersect, but a live area in which he can move around without disturbing the stage's balance). 'A' 'warms up' this area so as to bring it to life and then, when the time seems right, he moves away so as to unbalance the stage. 'B' then gets up and positions himself on stage in such a way as to realign it. From this moment on the game is joined and 'B' has the upper hand: he moves from one place to another, following his own personal rhythms and, each time he does so, 'A' must re-establish the balance by moving his position as well.

When he feels the need, 'A' can decide not to respond to the unbalancing movement of 'B', which once again disturbs the balance of the stage and calls for the entry of 'C'. This third player becomes the new leader of the game. 'A' and 'B' respond to his movements so as to maintain the balance, up until the point when, working together but without prior agreement, they too decide not to respond. This once again disturbs the balance and brings on a fourth player, etc. The game continues like this, with a growing number of actors, who constantly re-establish the balance disturbed by each new leader as soon as the others fail to respond.

Once this rule is thoroughly understood, which requires a long period of experimentation, we can enlarge the space (adding forty centimetres between each bench). More importantly, we can pay more attention to the quality of the game, underlining the notions of time and space. A secret bond establishes itself between watchers and players, not consisting of a direct relationship between them, but of a shared sense of being present in the space. Seated on the benches, all the participants can tell if the timing and placing of the players is right. They instinctively know when it is too long or too short, and whether the positions taken up are the right ones. This awareness is there among the watchers, who assist the players, by their very presence, to achieve the right timings and placings. They see the mistake of someone who thinks he can enter the stage although there is in fact no place for him. Besides, these errors are necessary and have to be allowed for if the game is to continue, for distance and timing cannot be reduced to mathematical precision.

We notice that actors instinctively take up positions which correspond to a simple geometry, linked to their number. When there are three of them, they tend to form an equilateral triangle; four a square, five a circle. These positions, which we already noted in the silent psychological improvisations, do not make for a playable dramatic situation. They can only find justification in rituals tending towards the monumental. Hence the research for a different distribution of positions, with rhythms which can breathe life into dramatic situations. An actor on the edge of the stage carries more weight than when he is central and so a variable distribution is required to maintain a balanced stage. The point of the game is gradually to achieve a harmonious relationship with time, space and the other actors on stage.

Next we try out different dramatic actions, according to the positions taken up by the actors. The situation is determined by the spatial relationship between them. Words can be brought in when the actors are static. The interplay between the actors can be direct when they are all looking at one another, or indirect if they are looking elsewhere. In this way we stage an unwritten play. Balancing the stage is the fundamental exercise for productions.

$1 = 1 + 1 \ldots$

A second rule, which follows on from the first, allows for the birth of a chorus and its leader, facing the hero. In the first rule each actor was of the same weight (1 = 1); in the second, the actor who enters is balanced by the weight of all the others (1 = 1 + 1 ...). The game begins in the same way: 'A' comes on, then brings on 'B', who becomes leader. 'A' then decides to bring on 'C', and at this moment the rule changes. Once he has found his point of balance, 'C' waits for 'A' and 'B' to get together in a balancing position. From this point on, 'A' plus 'B' together have the same weight as 'C'. Each new actor who comes on will cause those already on stage to regroup, up to the point when the eighth to come on will be leading a group of seven. He will be the first hero, facing the first chorus.

When he decides, the hero will fall to the ground, and this will be the signal for the chorus to break up. Six actors withdraw from the space, leaving one, motionless, facing the hero: this is the chorus leader, who has been placed there by the chorus and who will have the right to speak in the name of them all. I insist on the chorus leader being chosen by the others as they withdraw: it is not he who decides to take on the function by stepping forward. This precise moment of the exercise is particularly difficult and requires from all the actors a great sensitivity to one another. We often see two would-be chorus leaders left facing the hero: two is one too many.

Balancing the stage demands a very high level of concentration; the exercise cannot be sustained for more than an hour at a time. Numerous variants can be brought in, with different playing styles going from the most everyday realism to masked transformations. Certain deviations always attract my attention: 'the person who leads in someone else's place'; 'the person who robs someone else of his entrance'; 'the person who believes, mistakenly, that he is in the right place'; 'the person who won't give up his place'; 'the person who has no sense of time passing'; 'the person who hesitates and finds his place is taken'; 'the person who comes on stage when there is no place for him', etc. Each of these deviations produces a small disturbance of the balance and upsets the game.

I have had the opportunity to apply this chorus work in a variety of circumstances, notably with Jean Vilar[30] at the Théâtre National

Populaire, when he was playing the chorus leader in *Antigone*. When I was assisting with the production, Vilar asked me where he should position himself, and I suggested that he should remain at the back of the stage, concealed among the chorus, so as to appear with all the more force when the chorus disappeared. I had done something similar in Italy with the review *Who's on Stage?*. The opening tableau had the whole company of about sixty actors, all singing and dancing in an evocation of popular festivities in Rome. Suddenly the warning siren taken from Rossellini's[31] *Rome, Open City* blared out. The crowd disappeared leaving the great Anna Magnani alone, centre stage, dressed in a little black skirt and singing a song from Trastevere, one of Rome's working-class districts. Wonderful memories!

In tragedy men come face to face with divine laws and with destiny. They are not responsible for their actions, which are in the hands of the gods. Human passions, lust for power, hatred, love, jealousy, all run counter to the will of the gods and lead the heroes to their deaths. The people are always present, watching and commenting on these events. Although we were able to breathe life into the chorus, the question of the hero was much trickier. Once we had decided that we would not be restricted by the ancient models, that we rejected the traditional, monumental conception of the tragic hero, how were we to find a character sufficiently strong to balance a moving chorus in today's world? Who is the hero-figure of our time? In the course of the last twenty years, our search for the humanity of this character has led us down many different paths.

Paradoxically, it was melodrama that produced the modern hero. The man in the street, living alone in the simplest, most ordinary way, became the hero (or anti-hero) for our tragic chorus. The students felt the need to surround this everyday character with a chorus, which also included a few *bouffons*. The character could not see the people around him, but he was given support and advice by this chorus, who helped him, spoke to him, expressed his own internal voices. This melodramatic anti-hero introduced the great theme of solitude which links melodrama to tragedy at a profound level. The chorus filled the void which was left by solitude in a very human way. We had begun to open a door.

The necessity of text

The tragic dimension must be approached through texts, whether they be ancient or modern, not only texts written specifically for choruses but also other texts which enable us to reach a heightened expressive register. Of course I use the great plays of Aeschylus, Sophocles, Euripides, but also Racine or, closer to us, Antonin Artaud, Botho Strauss,[32] Michel Azama,[33] Steven Berkoff. I also use this magnificent text of the tragedy of nature written by Leonardo da Vinci, in which he described the dynamics of the Flood, before he painted it.

Our objective is not to work towards a finished production, but to concentrate on the constitution of the chorus and the physical and vocal work it demands. In our way of working, we enter a text through the body. We never sit round and discuss, but adopt the mimodynamic method. In the same way as we did for music and poetry, we explore the different texts: working through movement, we ask the actors to get to grips physically with the text, its images, its words, its dynamics. Relating to it does not involve interpreting it. To interpret it means to shed light on its different aspects, such as its period, context, society, psychology or morality. It is the director's responsibility to decide which aspects to emphasise. My teaching method steers clear of any interpretation, concentrating on the constant respect for the internal dynamics of the text, avoiding all *a priori* readings.

As a first stage, we make gestures as we speak the text, without worrying about its structure. All kinds of gestures emerge. The purpose of this basic work is to set the text free inside the body, so that the body does not become an obstacle. Once the text is learned, we strengthen the gestural dynamics, which are performed alone, in silence. Gradually the structure of the text takes shape after its cloudy beginnings.

Oh, what terrible sounds can be heard in the darkness, torn by the fury of the thunder and the brilliance of the lightning, striking and destroying everything in their path! Oh, how many wretches can be seen stopping their ears to avoid hearing the terrible roaring noise which fills the darkness with the fury of wind and rain, thunder from heaven and the lightning's rage! Others can be seen who, not content with closing their eyes, cover them with clenched hands to avoid seeing the cruel destiny visited on the human race by the anger of God. Oh, what transports of despair, what crowds of maddened people, hurling themselves from the rocks! The branches of a great oak can be seen laden with bodies blown there by the violence of the wind.

Every ship has been overturned, some intact, others in pieces, while the men struggle for safety, feeling the menace of approaching death. Others, despairing of being able to bear such pain, are committing suicide: some throw themselves from the rocks, others strangle themselves with their own hands; others seize their children and throw them down from the banks; others strike themselves with their own weapons; others fall to their knees and commend themselves to God.

Oh! how many mothers are weeping for drowned sons, whom they hold on their laps, lifting their arms to heaven and cursing the divine anger in screaming voices; others, their hands clenched together, bite cruelly into their own flesh as if they would devour themselves, or pray desperately, crushed by the immensity of their unbearable suffering.

> Leonardo da Vinci, *Codex Vaticanus*,
> Paris: Delagrave, 1910 (trans. D.B.)

HECUBA: Cursed soul!
Up from the earth.
Open your eyes ... look ...
Over there the city gone,
You are Queen of Troy no longer.
Change is the way of all things.
Accept it ...
Accept being swept away on the tide of the world,
Accept being dragged by the swell ...
Don't steer into the wave
The tiny vessel of your life ...
Cast life adrift!
Hecuba!
I want only the freedom to shout how it hurts,
When my homeland disappears,
My children,
And king.
My people bulging up
Like a sail filled by the wind,
My people vanishing ...
Who never were!
Do they demand my silence?
Or tell me to shout?
The weight of sorrow only released
By cries upon cries.
I let my heavy body sink
To the hard earth,
To sense where the pain is,
Through my head,
My breast,
My waist.
Let this body of mine be the hull of a ship,
Gently rocked by the swell,
Leaning slowly to the left,
Up and leaning to the left,
Swaying to the wake chanted by the dead.

Translated by David Wiles from the French text of
Jacqueline Moatti: a free translation of Euripides,
Trojan Women, lines 98–119

Next we work on improving the quality of the gestures, then, in small 'domes', made up of five to seven students standing in a circle, we look for the most appropriate gestures while speaking in chorus. One student, chosen as the best mimer of his group, stands in the centre and conducts the words of the chorus, which the others speak without moving. Working from gestures to immobility, the text is learned.

The second part of the work involves choices about how to alternate different voices so as to bring out the light and shade of the text, still without worrying about interpreting its meaning. The third stage is when I ask them to work in their *auto-cours* on a presentation of the chosen text, either motionless, or on the move, or with expressive gestures.

'Cast life adrift! Hecuba!' – and the whole chorus is carried away on a drifting movement, borne by Hecuba's cry, searching for rhythm, movement and intonation. The objective is not to discover some choreographic solution for the movements of the chorus, but rather to attain the point where the actor remains still, having experienced in his body the dynamics of the emotion and of the whole dramatic development. When an actor has been through these exercises and recites this text, in their mind's eye, his audience will see him move, even when he stands still.

When the students have explored a few short texts, and know them, we work on voice.

> A wave, high as a mountain, rears up, approaches, falls
> Crashing upon the shore, and spews, in eddying surf,
> A monster such as never has been seen on earth.
> Half-bull, half-dragon, horned, with leprous yellow scales,
> Its body coiled around in tortuous fetid trails.
> Bellowing, lurching forward, it shakes the troubled shores;
> The winds shriek in the sky in horror at its roars.

> Racine, *Phèdre* (trans. Robert David MacDonald),
> lines 1457–62 in *Landmarks of French Classical Drama*,
> Methuen, 1991

The furious monster of Théramène's account cannot be expressed using a small voice which comes from the head. The whole body has to be committed to understanding tragic fury. The actor may be assisted by others who pull him or push him or restrain him so that he may feel in his body the dynamics of the text. Using this kind of exercise, adapted to the particular needs of each text, we discover that the voice will develop into a genuine body voice, and this alone can convey the true tragic dimension. The actors will retain the trace of this physical relationship with the text. They will have embodied it before they come to think about interpretations.

We also work on the group voice of the chorus. The tragic chorus speaks with a single voice and the group of actors has to be able to achieve this collective dimension. For ensemble speaking, different techniques are used: one student recites a text that all have learned, another tries to speak the same text through the mouth of the first; gradually others join in until they achieve a common group voice, each member of the group having the impression that he is spoken by the others. This group voice is often moving and extremely beautiful. Sadly, it is seldom present in contemporary productions which often restrict the chorus to three or four actors, no doubt for financial reasons.

The international dimension of the school brings foreign actors into contact with French texts. It is interesting to observe how an attention to careful articulation brings out the force of the writing. The pains these students must take to rediscover the value of the words reap rich rewards. Several recent examples of foreign actors performing in French productions have shown the value of this procedure in productions by Antoine Vitez,[34] Peter Brook, Ariane Mnouchkine,[35] etc. For this work to have a successful outcome, play texts have to provide actors with something which they can sense physically, not just with their heads. This bodily presence is apparent in verbs which encourage or deny physical involvement. Of course not all texts are suitable for such work. Those of Ionesco

The Main Dramatic Territories

The YOUNG BOY *and the* YOUNG GIRL *are in an empty space, darkness all around.*

GIRL: Rrrr-iiii-pppp! (*She pulls an arm off her doll*) My doll's lost an arm in the bombing.

BOY: Quick! You have to burn the wound so it won't bleed.

GIRL: Silly! It's a doll. Dolls don't bleed.

BOY: You have to burn them all the same. You do it like this. (*He cauterises the doll's shoulder with a match*) It stinks. Plastic stinks just like people do when you burn them.

GIRL: My doll's a nice doll. Careful! She was hit by shrapnel. Rrrr-iiii-pppp! Rrrr-iiii-pppp! A leg and now her other arm!

BOY: Stop it. You'll end up killing her.

GIRL: Burn! Go on – burn! Oh, what a brilliant stink! You can get rid of everything – she won't die as long as it's not the head.

BOY: Maybe, but –

GIRL: But once you get rid of the head she dies. Oh! . . . Look! (*A tiny parachute falls from the flies*)

BOY: What is it?

GIRL: Looks like a present! A treat!

BOY: It's mine!

GIRL: No. It's mine.

BOTH: (*Fighting over the package*) 's mine. 's mine.

BOY: I'm stronger than you.

GIRL: You're silly. Silly like all boys. I bet there isn't anything good in that present. Medicine and rubbish like that.

BOY: You're jealous.

GIRL: No I'm not.

BOY: Yes you are.

GIRL: No I'm not.

BOY: Yes you are. Good. So if you're not jealous why are you crying? Shall I open it?

GIRL: I don't care. I'm looking after my doll or else she'll turn all black like my cousin did when he lost his arm.

BOY: Look. It's a truck. A petrol truck. Oh! It's got a remote!

GIRL: I don't care. It's silly. It's a boy's toy.

BOY: Listen. Don't be cross. Look. I put the truck down here. Right here next to me. And I give you this to steer it with. You press this button – right? – and the truck will come towards you. Okay? You're not still cross, are you? Will you play with me?

GIRL: Good. Yes. Give it here. (*The* BOY *is several yards from the* GIRL. *She presses the remote control button. The truck explodes. The* BOY *turns a somersault and falls lifeless to the ground.*)

GIRL: What are you doing? Hey, isn't it a good toy? Hey, what is this toy? Hey, you're not dead are you?

Michel Azama, *Crossfire* (trans. Nigel Gearing),
London: Oberon, 1993, pp. 20–1.

and Pinter do not draw on the whole body but remain located largely in the head. Beckett stands apart: his work 'breathes'. The greatest theatre involves the whole body: pelvis, solar plexus and head.

In the preceding prologue to his play *Crossfire*, Michel Azama adapts the *botta e risposta* of the *commedia dell'arte* for a tragic purpose. The condensation of dialogue moves the situation towards its dénouement through action in the present. Many of the school's students have gone on to become writers. I would not venture to claim that they became writers because of the school, but perhaps it has led them to write differently. Some say so. For my part, I recognise myself in their writing insofar as it differentiates between 'speech' [*le discours*] and 'the Word' [*la parole*]. Where 'speech' is stuck at the verbal level, 'the Word' involves the whole body. The territory of tragedy provides the most powerful demonstration of this.

Clowns

Finding one's own clown

The work of the school ends in laughter, with clowns and comic varieties: burlesques, eccentrics, all kinds of absurdities. With time, this territory has opened up more and more, becoming as important and as extensive as that of the neutral mask. Together, they frame the teaching offered by the school. To start with, this part of the work lasted for only two or three days; now it spreads over several weeks, as the students' fascination with the area has led me to delve into it more thoroughly.

Clowns first appeared in the 1960s, when I was investigating the relationship between the *commedia dell'arte* and circus clowns. My main discovery came in answer to a simple question: the clown makes us laugh, but how? One day I suggested that the students should arrange themselves in a circle – recalling the circus ring – and make us laugh. One after the other, they tumbled, fooled

The solitude of the clown

around, tried out puns, each one more fanciful than the one before, but in vain! The result was catastrophic. Our throats dried up, our stomachs tensed, it was becoming tragic. When they realised what a failure it was, they stopped improvising and went back to their seats feeling frustrated, confused and embarrassed. It was at that point, when they saw their weaknesses, that everyone burst out laughing, not at the characters that they had been trying to show us, but at the person underneath, stripped bare for all to see. We had the solution. The clown doesn't exist aside from the actor performing him. We are all clowns, we all think we are beautiful, clever and strong, whereas we all have our weaknesses, our ridiculous side, which can make people laugh when we allow it to express itself. During our first experiences of this, I noticed that there were students with legs so thin that they hardly dared show them, but who found, in playing the clown, a way to exhibit their skinniness for the pleasure of the onlookers. At last they were free to be as they were, and to make people laugh. This discovery of how personal weakness can be transformed into dramatic strength was the key to my elaboration of a personal approach to clowning, involving a search for 'one's own clown', which became a fundamental principle of the training.

The reference to circus, which is bound to surface as soon as clowns are mentioned, remains marginal, in my view. As a child, I saw the Fratellini brothers, Grock, the Carioli trio, Portos and Carletos, all at the Médrano circus in Montmartre, but we were not after this kind of clown at the school. Apart from the comic register, we took no external models, either formal or stylistic, and the students themselves had no knowledge of the clowns I have mentioned. They thus embarked on their research in complete freedom and it was Pierre Byland, a student at the school before he returned to teach here, who first introduced the famous red nose, the smallest mask in the world, which would help people to expose their naivety and their fragility.

Research on one's own clown begins by looking for one's

ridiculous side. Unlike in *commedia dell'arte*, there is no pre-established character to support the actor (e.g. Harlequin, Pantalone, etc.), so he has discover the clown part within himself. The less defensive he is, the less he tries to play a character, and the more he allows himself to be surprised by his own weaknesses, the more forcefully his clown will appear.

> *You enter very conscious of your strength; you are handsome, clever, you arrive as a conqueror. You go to do something which is important in your eyes for demonstrating this strength and superiority ... but you cannot manage it! The ring-master, acting as referee, asks you what is the matter? Are you sure you can do it? Have you practised hard? Are you doing it for the first time? Or have you just worked with amateurs?*

In response to these questions the actor must play the truth game: the more he is himself, the more his weakness is shown up, the funnier he will be. Above all he must avoid playing a role, but give free rein, in the most psychological manner, to the innocence inside him which comes out when he is a flop or bungles his presentation.

It is impossible to list themes for clowns: the whole of life is a clown theme, if you are a clown. When the actor comes on stage wearing a small red nose, his face is in a state of openness, entirely without defence. He thinks he will be sympathetically welcomed by the audience (the world), and he is surprised to be greeted by silence when he was convinced that he is a very important person. His pitiful reaction sets a few spectators laughing. The clown, who is ultra-sensitive to others, reacts to everything that happens to him and varies between a sympathetic smile and an expression of sadness. In this first contact with an audience, the teacher must watch whether the actor precedes his intentions. He should always be in a state of reaction and surprise, without letting his performance be deliberately led (we say 'telephoned'), reacting before he has any motive for doing so.

The clown is the person who flops, who messes up his turn, and, by so doing, gives his audience a sense of superiority. Through his failure he reveals his profoundly human nature, which moves us and makes us laugh. But he cannot flop with just anything, he has to mess up something he knows how to do, that is to say an exploit. I ask each student to choose something which only he, out of the whole class, can manage: the splits, finger contortions, a special whistle. The virtuosity of the action is unimportant; it is only an exploit if no one else is able to do it. Clown work then consists in establishing a relationship between the exploit and the flop. Ask a clown to do a somersault: he fails. Give him a kick in the backside and he does it without realising. In both cases he makes us laugh. If he never succeeds, we are tipping over into the tragic.

As always, the pedagogic process for the approach to clown work is developmental. We begin with a session devoted to bad taste in which we are as uninhibited as possible (we call it 'going over the top').

> You are to put on a disguise, as if you were going to a fancy-dress party. A trunk is brought in with all kinds of props and costumes. Everyone puts on a false beard or moustache or a funny hat and enjoys themselves in total freedom.

Disguising themselves liberates the actors from their social mask. They are free to do 'what they want' and this freedom can produce unsuspected personal behaviour. Gradually we remove the disguise so as to reach the clown with the addition of the red nose, which is used in the exercise called 'Discovering the Audience':

> Someone comes on stage and discovers the audience.

This exercise obliges the actor to enter directly into the clown dimension. The great difficulty consists in finding this dimension from the start, genuinely playing himself, and not 'playing the clown'. If he starts to make a performance out of his own personal silly side, the actor is lost. You cannot play at being a clown; you are one, when your deep nature surfaces in the first fears of childhood.

Unlike theatre characters, the contact the clown has with his public is immediate, he comes to life by playing with the people who are looking at him. It is not possible to be a clown *for* an audience; you play *with* your audience. As the clown comes on stage, he establishes contact with all the people making up his audience and their reactions influence his playing. This is an important exercise for the trainee actor because it enables him to experience a strong, lively relationship with an audience. If the clown took no notice of audience reactions, he would become trapped in his 'flop' and would end up in a psychiatric ward. I once asked the great comic actor Raymond Devos to come and give a special class on the clown. He did a masterly improvisation prompted by the leg of a chair being put down on his foot. The smallest reaction, a movement, a laugh, a single word from his audience was used by him to take off in a new direction. It was an impressive display of great clowning.

A parallel search involves looking for ways of walking that are buried deep within us. Watching the way each person walks, we can pick out the characteristic features (one arm swinging more than the other, feet which point inwards, a slightly protruding belly, a head leaning to one side) and then exaggerate them progressively until we reach a personal transposition. I help the students to research their own clown walk, just as Groucho Marx, Charlie Chaplin or Jacques Tati all had their characteristic walks. It is never a question of the clown building something external, always a gradual development of their own, personal walk.

At the same time, we do technical work on forbidden gestures, the ones which an actor has never been able to express in society. 'Walk properly!', 'Stand up straight!', 'Stop scratching your head!' – such are the injunctions that lead us to keep certain gestures buried deep in our childhood bodies without ever allowing ourselves to express them. This is work of a very psychological nature and gives the actor great freedom in his playing. It is useful for the students to experience this freedom, finding themselves stripped of all defences, in what I call the primary clown.

References to circus return when we come to the phenomenon of the trio. Circus clowns often come in threes: the white-face clown, the Auguste and the second Auguste. A pecking order is a necessary part of any clown situation. This is obvious in the famous trio of the Marx Brothers, but it is also a feature of duos: Harlequin and Brighella, Laurel and Hardy, etc. One is always the butt of the other. In the theatre the duo seems preferable, since it is desirable, in a teaching situation, for each clown to learn to situate himself in relation to another. This research on pecking orders is followed up especially in the exercise of 'The Practical Joke' and 'The Double Flop'.

> *The white-face clown plays a practical joke on the first Auguste. He asks him to bend over, to pick something up. The Auguste does so, and the clown takes the opportunity to give him a kick in the backside. The clown then starts to laugh and the Auguste laughs too, as he struggles to save his face.*
>
> *The second Auguste comes by. The first Auguste tries to play the same trick on him and asks him to bend over. The second Auguste knows the score and is not taken in, so he pretends not to understand. In an attempt to explain what he wants, the first Auguste bends over ... and gets a second kick in the backside. Double flop!*

When I introduced work on clowns, I thought it would be a temporary stage, a phase in our search for new teaching methods, linked to a particular period. Today I notice that the students are always asking to work on clowns and consider it one of the high points of the school's educational journey. No doubt clowns put us in touch with a very profound psychological and theatrical dimension. They have become as important as the neutral mask, but working in reverse. While the neutral mask is all-inclusive, a common denominator which can be shared by all, the clown brings out the individual in his singularity. He gives the lie to everybody's claim to be better than the next person. Paradoxically, this brings us to a limit at the opposite end from the direction of most of our pedagogic methods. For months on end I have been asking the students to observe the world and allow it to be reflected in them. With the clown, I ask them to be themselves as profoundly as they possibly can, and to observe the effect they produce on the world, that is to say their audience. This gives them the experience of freedom and authenticity in front of an audience.

The clown needs no conflicts because he is in a permanent state of conflict, notably with himself. This phenomenon demands care and attention from the teacher so as to avoid pseudo-psycho-analytic interpretations of the difficult psychological process the actors have to undergo. The students must be prevented from becoming too caught up in playing their own clown, since it is the dramatic territory which brings them into closest contact with their own selves. In fact the clown should never be hurtful for the actor. The audience does not directly make fun of him; they feel superior and laugh, which is quite different. Moreover, the actor is masked, partly protected by the little red nose. Most important, this work comes at the end of their two years in the school, when the students are used to investing themselves fully in their playing, used to knowing and showing themselves in front of others. This is not always the case in the innumerable short workshops on clowning which are offered here and there, and which can only give a very superficial, reductive approach to work which needs to be prepared for in all the previous stages.

I like this work to be undertaken at the end of the course because you can only be a clown when you have built up an experience of life. In the circus tradition, the clowns are usually drawn from among the older artists. The young ones are working on such exploits as tightrope walking, trapeze or balancing acts which the older ones can no longer manage, so they become clowns, expressing their maturity, their wisdom!

In their *auto-cours* the students prepare a turn which they are assumed to have performed with great success in a far-off country, and which will, of course, flop. They search out a suitable costume, starting with clothes that are too big or too small, so that this is already their first failure: a hat which won't stay on, socks which are too long, trousers which are too short, etc. After this they try out their 'flop' which can be presented in one of two ways. The first is the 'pretentious flop', when the clown performs a pathetic turn while believing it to be brilliant: the greatest turn of the century is announced and, when he comes on, all he can do is to juggle with three balls. The second is the 'accidental flop', where the clown fails to do what he attempts: he fails to hold his balance on a stool, or falls over while making a simple jump, etc.

The next stage of the work is to put clowns into everyday situations. We work on families of clowns: father, mother, children. The clowns move house … go on holiday … look for work, etc. We also use exercises which are at the limits of fiction and reality, for example, 'The Clowns Rehearse a Play'. It's not a matter of performing the play in a clowning style, but of clowns who really want to rehearse but cannot manage it. So many things happen that they never get round to rehearsing the play, all we get are disasters and unexpected exploits. In each of these situations, each clown emerges clearly, in his ridiculous aspect and sometimes in his tragic dimension.

Comic varieties: the burlesque, the absurd

Finally I ask the students to put on a show using all these experiments and to create a genuine clown sequence, devised and rehearsed as they choose. This final show brings out the personal quality of each of the students, their peculiar fantasies and imaginative worlds. The performances may follow a number of different pathways, presenting clowns (with or without red noses), burlesque, absurd or eccentric characters. In addition, the international dimension of the school emphasises the differences, from one country to another, in what makes people laugh. What seems funny to the English does not necessarily make an Italian or a Japanese laugh, but clowns from whatever country must be able to make the whole world laugh. Some elements of laughter are analysed from the technical point of view. The double image is an example. In one of Jacques Tati's films, Monsieur Hulot is repairing his car, pumping up a tyre, which runs away and rolls down an autumn street. Dead leaves stick to the tyre and it finishes up in a cemetery. Hulot picks it up and then finds himself in the middle of a funeral, carrying what looks like a wreath. This is pure association of ideas and double image. It is a technique frequently used by Charlie Chaplin: he is being chased, so he puts a lampshade on his head and pretends to be a lampstand.

Comic varieties are extensions of the work on clowns, marked by special characteristics. The burlesque relies on gags, more difficult to bring off in the theatre than in the cinema, for they often invert reality and come close to cartoons: the wood-cutter chops through a tree, but instead of falling, it flies away.

Three exhausted mountaineers discover three chairs, stagger towards them with great difficulty and, the moment they reach them . . . load them on their backs and continue climbing!

This theme, recently performed by our students, inverts reality and produces laughter.

The absurd makes use of two contradictory forms of logic. I ask the way of someone, who points out the road leading off to the right . . . I take the one that turns left! In fact, I am going back to get my suitcase, which justifies my left turn, but the person I asked (like the audience) does not know that. He cannot understand it and so the situation appears absurd to him.

The eccentric character does things differently from other people. His centre is elsewhere. He combs his hair . . . with a rake. Another eccentric is a virtuoso on the piano . . . which he plays with his toes.

Second-year clown presentation

This territory calls for practical skills such as acrobatics, juggling, music and singing. We work on clown movements: kicks and games with hats. We play with words, taking literally a phrase like 'night falls', with the clown looking for the place where it has fallen. Many of the students can play an instrument and every year we put together a band in the spirit of cabaret or review. I like the students to practise comic cabaret turns, working up short numbers, never longer than ten minutes. Sadly, all the places where young actors might present such work have disappeared and the post-war cabarets of Paris are long since gone. Today young performers are expected to come up straight away with a one-man show lasting an hour, which is far too difficult and ought to be the result of extensive research on shorter forms.

Although every student goes through the work on clowns, very few of them will continue in this register. A few are natural comics: they only have to walk on stage and everyone bursts out laughing. The purpose of our teaching is to enable them to discover who they are, to be themselves. The neutral mask and the clown frame a student's journey through the school, one at the beginning, the other at the end. As actors they will not retain these masks. They will venture out on their own creative paths, but the masks will have left their marks and their spirit. And the students will at last have experienced the fundamental reality of creation: solitude.

Structures depicting human passions

3

The Laboratory for the
Study of Movement [L.E.M.]

Since 1976 a department of experimental scenography has been added to the school, set up in collaboration with the architect Krikor Belekian. The course lasts for one year and is open to students from the school who have an interest in this area, as well as to people from outside: architects, scenographers, painters, etc. The L.E.M. [Laboratoire d'Etude du Mouvement] has two strands of work which complement one another, in line with the broad pedagogic approach of the school: movement work which brings the miming body into play, and creative work which involves building scenographic structures.

Any living space has 'dramatic possibilities' and influences the behaviour of the people who enter it or the characters who perform in it. A change of place modifies all our attitudes and behaviour, down to the pace at which we walk. We walk around differently on a visit to a Gothic church from the way we walk around a Romanesque church. Before constructing a habitable space, whether for real-life dramas or for those off the stage, it is important to work out in advance the life which will exist in the space. I remember one of my architectural students taking me to visit a mountain chalet on which construction work had not yet started. He brought the spaces to life for me as if we were in them: he basked in the light from a window, he walked through doors, climbed the stairs to the attic, stooped beneath the sloping roof. A few years later I visited the finished chalet – I already knew it inside out!

We introduce a preliminary sensitisation of the body to the spaces it inhabits, first in a neutral state, and then in dramatic expression. We work through replaying built spaces so as to be receptive to

165

our initial physical impressions, then go on to *mimages* in order to understand their dynamics (an observational *mimage* aimed at understanding reality and a pre-creative *mimage* with a view to future creations). This is yet another way of developing the profound sensitivity of the body towards the observation of reality.

In this work space the students progress from the study of human walking to an understanding of the laws of movement and the spaces of the body. They then study the human passions, from jealousy to pride, with reference to a state of calm. Lastly come the colours and their dynamics, their dimension and force, even the battle between them. After each one of these physical explorations, we return to the studio and ask the participants to create three-dimensional objects which embody their discoveries (e.g. structures and forms built from basic materials such as wood, cardboard, string, clay, etc.). These objects develop into costumes, masks, model-boxes.

The year's course at the L.E.M. concludes with specific projects. For this the participants create a scenographic presentation based on a theme. This may have a direct relationship to everyday life (a memory, a landscape, etc.), or may be inspired by a piece of music, poetry or literature, or something from the plastic arts (Stravinsky, Miró, Saint-John Perse,[36] *Don Quixote, The Divine Comedy, Faust,* etc.). Taking these themes, the students build portable structures, small models of theatrical spaces with no actors, or any other invention they choose to create movement in, not with the aim of illustrating something but simply to research the internal dynamics which they can show in the space.

Taking *Hamlet* as a theme would obviously not involve learning how to construct the set for the first act, but rather showing the future scenographer how spaces must be constructed which *await* the drama to be played out. When he inscribes in space the scenography of *Hamlet,* the space itself will hold the density of the drama. He will have understood that performances are not given in front of a set, but in a dynamic construction where the actors can play with the space.

Every dramatic theme needs a space specially adapted for its performance. The miming body explores the themes of a drama in an empty space, so as to understand their underlying movements. Starting from there, one can begin to construct the optimum space in which they can be played out.

In this way the L.E.M. develops a particular view of the movement of a space, closely related to the performance of the actors. It teaches how to construct the invisible, how to give body and movement to things which seem to have none. The experience of the L.E.M course is very practical and no written explanation could do it justice. It brings each student face to face with himself.

The teaching is based on certain points of reference: balance, the state of calm, the fixed point, the economy of physical actions. These terms must not be seen as absolutes, but must be allowed a certain flexibility, leaving room for a sense of humour. Calm is maintained by two conflicting forces in opposition. Balance can be seen in motion. The fixed point is able to move around itself without being lost. The economy of physical actions is a discovery made afresh in the body of each student.

There is no movement without a fixed point. If it cannot be found, it must be invented!

IV

NEW BEGINNINGS

The teaching methods developed at the school in the course of these last forty years have given rise to offshoots of all kinds around the world. Both in the field of dramatic writing (in the broadest sense of the term, including authors, but also the originators of performances without text), and in the fields of performance, directing or scenography, former students have created productions that belong to their time. I won't single out individuals here – I would have to cite them all, famous and unknown alike – and I leave it up to each person to credit the teaching he has received should he wish to.

Sometimes groups have formed following the end of the second year, and have set themselves up as companies, preferring to pursue the collaborative work begun during their time at the school rather than to join existing theatres. This seems to me especially significant for the new young theatre which I hope to see come into existence. Looking back, I recall especially the work of the Mummenschantz whose research into masks and forms has been far-reaching. The Footsbarn Travelling Theatre, set up in Cornwall before they emigrated to the Auvergne, worked to rediscover the authenticity of the greatest texts. The Moving Picture Mime Show brought cartoon mime to a wider public. The Théâtre de la Jacquerie explored society through the grotesque. The Nada Théâtre developed a creative poetic use of objects. Theatre de Complicite evolved a new stage language for today's theatre. Not forgetting the Theatre de la Jeune Lune at Minneapolis, and so many others who have followed similar paths.

The school's teaching methods have also been exported to a number of countries. Schools based on our method of teaching have been set up in Bologna, Brussels, Milan, London, Madrid, Barcelona, etc. From the Conservatoire of Québec to the Royal

Scottish Academy in Glasgow, by way of Japan, Chile and Australia, many former students have, in their turn, taken up the teaching and developed it according to their own vision. Above and beyond a particular method, we are united by the pioneering aspect of the teaching, which points towards the theatre of the future. A theatre school should not always journey in the wake of existing theatre forms. On the contrary, it should have a visionary aspect, developing new languages of the stage and thus assisting in the renewal of theatre itself. This is what we have achieved with our rediscovery of masks, the chorus, clowns, *bouffons*, etc., all of which have enriched innumerable new performances.

Since the school pays more attention to creative than to interpretative work, since it prefers to encourage new writers rather than depend on existing plays, I am sometimes able to detect the shape of future dramatic developments. For this, I must retain my insistence on permanency while also being sensitive to developments suggested by young students. One has to keep moving on!

Every precise definition of pedagogic method, from my approach to the great dramatic territories onwards, suggests the need for combinations. Only by going beyond the frontiers, passing from one territory to another and overlapping them, can true creativity be nurtured and new territories come to light. The idea of 'pure' theatre is dangerous. What would 'pure' melodrama amount to? Or 'pure' tragedy? Purity is death! Chaos is necessary to creation, but 'chaos' must be organised, allowing each person to put down roots and develop his own creative rhythms.

Mime has not only opened itself up to the theatre, it has also had relevance for movement in general, and especially for dance. Certain choreographers have returned to the theatre in search of gestures which had been lost to the art of dance, and such encounters have been partially responsible for the renewal of modern dance. Research undertaken in this spirit is a feature of, for example, the work of the Bouvier/Obadia company, founded by two former students.

Lastly, I would like to mention the potential value of mimodynamic methods for all sorts of areas of training, quite apart from
theatre, not only in the arts but in other disciplines too. I have
been able to apply this to the training of architects, not so that they
might become actors, but to improve their construction skills,
respecting the movements of the human body in space. Similar
applications could be made in other arts such as music and the
plastic arts – we have made a start on this – but also in literature,
dance, etc. The same pedagogic process can be adapted to all
artistic education; it means involving the miming body in the
recognition and understanding of reality, allowing each person to
embody the world around him before sitting down to paint it,
sing, dance or write about it. The resulting forms would, no doubt,
be more deeply felt and less cerebral.

The main difficulty we face is the contemporary fascination with
hi-tech gadgetry whose appeal is merely external, aesthetically
spurious and at the mercy of the latest fashion. There are theatre
productions whose sole aim is to make a stir and astonish the
public at any price. Young students are right to reject this type of
theatre. They are more interested in forms which are simpler, but
more powerful, because they are rooted in real life, which everyone
can understand. They seek truth in illusion, not in lies!

Besides, what brings them to the school? Why do so many young
artists, sometimes from the other side of the world, come to take
my classes? Can they not find something to satisfy them in their
own country? I often ask myself these questions, and the reply is
simple: they are in search of truth, authenticity, a foundation
which will outlive fashion. When they come with this aspiration, it
is up to me to respond with complete honesty, and no hint of
demagogy. They need to be met with words of strength, a
permanent reference point that will stay with them throughout
their creative lives.

GLOSSARY

Acting levels Starting from neutrality (see Neutrality) each different performance style is seen by Lecoq as having its own level. See p. 54.

Action mime See Mime.

Attitude A powerful moment of stasis, isolated within a movement. Lecoq isolates nine fundamental attitudes and provides a diagram. See pp. 72–80.

Auto-cours The name given to the one-and-a-half-hour sessions which take place each day at the school, when groups of students work on their own, without direct supervision by teachers. They prepare an improvisation based on themes established by Jacques Lecoq, and present their work in front of the whole school at the end of each week. See 'The Students' Own Theatre', pp. 96–9.

Botta e risposta Traditional *commedia dell'arte* technique of quick-fire dialogue, often consisting of only a word or two per character as illustrated on p. 122.

Bouffons Performance style drawing on elements of the grotesque, parody, fantasy and mystery. See pp. 124–34.

Cartoon mime See Mime.

Character mask See Expressive mask.

Complicity A term used by Lecoq to mean shared understanding between two actors (e.g. p. 34) or between actors and audience. It was seen as a key term by Simon McBurney and the founders of Theatre de Complicite (all former pupils of Lecoq, the company originally called itself Théâtre de Complicité).

Constraints The imposition of, for example, a very restricted space on a group of actors attempting to portray action taking place over very wide distances. See pp. 67–8.

Counter-mask See Mask.

Detour, Deviation, Digression   Terms used to translate Lecoq's word *dérive*, a term which he uses to indicate anything which branches off from the neutral state. See pp. 32, 61.

Disequilibrium   This designates the origin of all motion (see p. 94). Disequilibrium and Progression are one of three linked pairs used in the exploration of movement technique as set out on pp. 78–9.

Dramatic acrobatics   Different movements drawing an acrobatic exercises which take their place in dramatic sequences. See pp. 73–4.

Dramatic gymnastics   Exercises originating in the discipline of gymnastics which are put to use in developing acting students' physical and vocal abilities. See pp. 70–3.

Dramatic Territories   See Territories.

Driving forces   See Motors (of play).

Dynamic geometry   The arrangement of groupings on stage that avoid the inert precision of the military parade ground (see pp. 139–40), achieving organic rhythm (see p. 33).

Eclosion   A scientific term used for one of the movements drawn from nature explained in the section entitled Movement Analysis. See p. 78 for explanation, p. 76 for diagram.

Equilibrium   The terms Equilibrium and Respiration are used by Lecoq to designate the extreme limits of all movement applicable to the performance of the actor. The point of Equilibrium is the point of extreme expansion; its opposite 'consists simply of respiration, in apparent immobility'. See p. 79.

Essence, Essential, Essentialise   Lecoq's verb *essentialiser* means to reduce any movement or action to its essential components, usually understood in an abstract or poetic sense. See pp. 40, 47.

Exploit   The opposite of a Flop (see below), an action requiring special skill. See p. 156.

Expressive mask   See Mask.

Fantastic   The fantastic is one of three distinct, almost separate territories to emerge in the course of work on *bouffons*. The others are mystery and the grotesque. See pp. 127–9.

Figurative mime   see Mime.

Flop   An attempted Exploit (see above) which fails utterly and miserably but produces laughter in the process. Lecoq's concept of the Flop is fundamental to his analysis of the clown. See p. 156.

Geodramatics   Neologism invented by Lecoq (in French: *géodramatique*) to convey the nature of the second year of the course, in which the school's exploration of acting employs many metaphors drawn from geology and geography (e.g. territories). See pp. 103–6.

Grotesque   The grotesque is one of three distinct, almost separate territories to emerge in the course of work on *bouffons*. The others are mystery and the fantastic. See pp. 127–9.

Identifications   Third phase of work with neutral mask, in which students identify themselves with the elements of water, fire, air, earth. See pp. 42–5, 87.

Indications   One of the three ways of justifying a movement listed on p. 69; the other two are action and states.

Inverse undulation   See Undulation.

Investigations   Practical research projects undertaken by the students outside the school, investigating some aspect of contemporary life. See p. 97.

Larval mask   See Mask.

L.E.M.   This stands for Laboratoire d'Etude du Mouvement (Laboratory for the Study of Movement) and is the name given to a separate, one-year course, originally intended for scenographers and designers, but which has broadened out to include the study of all aspects of theatre, based on the same principles of human movement as the other work of the school. See pp. 165–7.

Levels of acting, levels of playing, levels of performance   See Acting levels.

Lines of force Geometrical term borrowed by Lecoq to indicate the basis of redefiniton of character. See p. 64.

Mask

character mask See expressive mask.

counter-mask A mask which is played for the opposite of what it appears to represent. See p. 61.

expressive mask A mask representing a particular character. Also named 'character mask'. See pp. 54–9.

larval mask Masks representing semi-formed faces inspired by those used in the carnival at Basel in Switzerland. See p. 60 for illustration.

neutral mask 'A perfectly balanced mask which produces a physical sensation of calm. This object, when placed on the face, should enable one to experience the state of neutrality prior to action, a state of receptiveness to everything around us, with no inner conflict. This mask is a reference point, a basic mask, a fulcrum mask for all the other masks.' (See pp. 36–42).

noble mask The name given by Jacques Copeau and his disciples to what Jacques Lecoq later developed into the neutral mask. See p. 5.

utilitarian mask A mask created for a particular use, e.g. a solderer's mask, an ice-hockey player's face-guard, etc. See p. 61.

Mime

action mime The foundation for the analysis of human physical action. See pp. 82–4.

cartoon mime Performance technique drawing on cinematic effects. See p. 108.

figurative mime The use of the performer's body to represent physical objects. See p. 108.

melomime A technique combining melodramatic imagery with cartoon mime (explained above). See p. 115.

mimage Neologism which collapses in a single term the two words 'mime' and 'image'. Lecoq defines the *mimage* as 'a kind of "close-up" on the character's internal dramatic state. Feelings are never performed or explained, but the actor produces lightning gestures which express, through a different logic, the character's state at a given moment.' See p. 109.

mimodynamic   A method allowing the actor to discover physical movements which translate into bodily action the sensations aroused in them by colours, words, music. See pp. 47–54.

open mime   Mime seen as the fundamental creative act. See p. 22.

storytelling mime   A technique which combines spoken narration with other silent forms of acting or gestural langauges. See p. 110.

Motors (of play)   Lecoq's term *moteur*, sometimes translated as 'driving force', is used to indicate the dynamic principles underlying dramatic representation. See pp. 104–5.

Mystery   One of three distinct, almost separate territories to emerge in the course of work on *bouffons*. The others are the fantastic and the grotesque. See pp. 127–9.

Neutrality, Neutral state   The state prior to action or character creation, when the actor is in a state of perfect balance, presenting nothing but a neutral generic being. 'A character experiences conflict, has a history, a past, a context, passions. On the contrary, a neutral mask puts the actor in a state of perfect balance and economy of movement. Its moves have a truthfulness, its gestures and actions are economical. Movement work based on neutrality provides a series of fulcrum points which will be essential for acting, which comes later.' See pp. 38–9.

Neutral mask   See Mask.

Noble mask   See Mask.

Open mime   See Mime.

Pantomime   Type of performance in which gestures replace words because the actor accepts the contraint of not being able to use spoken language. White Pantomime conveys the style of silent performance common in the eighteenth and nineteenth centuries, when Pierrot became the central character and which was immortalised in the film *Les Enfants du Paradis*. See p. 107 for both Pantomime and White Pantomime.

Play Lecoq's conception of acting is founded on an approach that could be called playful or improvisatory. He exploits to the full the overlap of meanings contained in the words play and player, between child's play and drama, games and performances. His own definition of play is as follows: 'when the actor, aware of the theatrical dimension, can shape an improvisation for spectators, using rhythm, tempo, space, form'. See p. 29.

Replay In order to stress the importance of Play (see above) the term Replay is used to indicate a first stage in building up improvisation work. Replay involves reviving lived experience in the simplest possible way. See p. 29.

Respiration The terms Equilibrium and Respiration are used by Lecoq to designate the extreme limits of all movement applicable to the performance of the actor. The point of Equilibrium is the point of extreme expansion; its opposite 'consists simply of respiration, in apparent immobility'. See p. 79.

Rhythm An organic sense of movement not to be confused with Tempo: 'Tempo is geometrical, rhythm in organic. Tempo can be defined, while rhythm is difficult to grasp. Rhythm is the result of an actor's response to another live performer. It may be found in waiting, but also in action. To enter into the rhythm is, precisely, to enter into the great driving force of life itself. Rhythm is at the root of everything, like a mystery.' See p. 33.

Rose of effort A diagrammatic way of expressing the multidimensional aspects of movement. See pp. 85–6.

Scale Musical term used to convey different phases in the progression of a dramatic action. The principle of the scale is frequently used in the school, especially in exploring different levels of acting (see Acting levels).

States Term used to indicate the main orientation of a character and to avoid the actor relying on imitation of pre-existing models. See pp. 63–4, 69–70.

Storytelling mime See Mime.

Tempo   See Rhythm.

Territories Term used by Lecoq to designate the major dramatic genres of melodrama, tragedy, etc. The use of a metaphor invoking the need to travel links to his overall view of life (and the life of the school in particular) as a 'journey'.

Theme   Designates both the subject for an exercise and the exercise itself, especially when Lecoq asks students to work on certain situations that he regards as fundamental, such as 'Waiting' (p. 31), 'The Farewell' (p. 41), or 'The Exodus' (p. 97).

Traces   The result of work on identifications (see above), a form of body memory. See p. 46.

Transference   Method of going beyond the mere imitation of nature (see Transposing below). See pp. 45–6.

Transposing   The aim of much of Lecoq's training is to help the students achieve a level of theatrical transposition going beyond realistic performance (i.e. performance whose aim is merely to imitate the real world). See p. 45.

Undulation and **inverse undulation**   Two of the three natural movements observed in nature (the third is Eclosion). See pp. 75–8.

Universal poetic awareness   Term used to translate Lecoq's *le fonds poétique commun*, a concept with Jungian resonances, suggesting that all humans share a sensibility to an abstract dimension, made up of spaces, lights, colours, materials and sounds found in all of us. See pp. 47–8.

White pantomime   See Pantomime.

Zanni   Term used in *commedia dell'arte* for comic servants.

NOTES

1 The college attended by Lecoq was at Bagatelle, on the outskirts of Paris.

2 Antoine de Saint-Exupéry, well-known author of *Le Petit Prince* and novels which celebrated the exploits of pilots employed to fly dangerous routes in the early days of aviation.

3 Antonin Artaud, actor, director and visionary author of many volumes on the theatre of which the best known is *The Theatre and its Double*.

4 Jean-Louis Barrault, director and actor who enjoyed a reputation in the post-war French theatre similar to that of Sir Laurence Olivier in England.

5 This famous performance by Jean-Louis Barrault was part of his staging of Faulkner's novel *As I Lay Dying* in 1935. Barrault's depiction of man and horse moving as one was praised by Artaud in an essay reprinted in *The Theatre and its Double*.

6 Like that of Barrault, the other names mentioned here are those of avant-garde actors and directors – Roger Blin was to become the major exponent of both Beckett and Genet after the war; André Clavé was director of a touring company La Roulotte, founded in 1936, and became director of the Centre Dramatique de l'Est from 1947 to 1952; Marie-Hélène Dasté, the daughter of Jacques Copeau, married Jean Dasté and worked with both him and Barrault as actor and director; and Claude Martin was an 'animateur' and avant-garde director.

7 An influential organisation, first established as part of the cultural wing of the French Resistance movement, Travail et Culture aimed to develop opportunities for working-class people to develop their participation in artistic activities.

8 A celebrated director, one of a group of four who, inspired by the pioneering efforts of Jacques Copeau between 1913 and 1924, formed a 'cartel' in 1927 for the defence of a theatre dedicated to the highest artistic standards at a time when commercialisation was the rule and no theatres (apart from the Comédie Française) were subsidised.

9 The son-in-law of Jacques Copeau, Dasté was keen to work in decentralised theatre. After a few years at Grenoble, he founded the Comédie de Saint-Etienne, where he performed and directed for more than thirty years. He may have influenced Lecoq's concept of the

artistic journey – his autobiography was entitled *Voyage d'un comédien* [*Journey of an Actor*].

10 This was a punning name adopted by the group of trainee actors who followed Copeau when he retired from Paris to the provinces in 1924.

11 The term '*animateur dramatique*' suggests anyone who works to bring a theatre and its audience closer together in what would now he termed 'educational outreach'. After the upheavals of 1968, many young *animateurs* decided to abandon theatre for work in the community and the term became synonymous with politically motivated cultural agitation, but this is not the sense in which Lecoq uses it.

12 Pseudonym for Angelo Beolco, actor and playwright who lived in Padua in the first half of the sixteenth century and whose plays, many of which dramatise peasant life, are seen as precursers of the *commedia dell'arte*.

13 The world-famous Piccolo Teatro was founded in Milan in 1947 by Paolo Grassi and Giorgio Strehler. It was founded on a strong anti-Fascist ideology and made a priority of attracting working-class audiences. Its policies and programming had much in common with those of Jean Vilar in France, although it took a more overt political stance than Vilar's Théâtre National Populaire (see note 15).

14 Anna Magnani, the Italian actress who made her name in theatre, performing in both classic works and comic revues, and who went on to acquire an international reputation through her film performances, especially in Italian neo-realist films e.g. Rossellini's *Rome, Open City* (1945).

15 In the 1940s and 1950s Vilar was the director most responsible for developing a vision of popular theatre in France, a theatre performing both classic and contemporary work, dedicated to the highest artistic standards, but guaranteeing access to all. He founded the Avignon Theatre Festival in 1947 and, following its success, was appointed to head the Théâtre National Populaire in Paris in 1951. Under his direction, this rapidly acquired a very high reputation.

16 Gabriel Cousin, playwright, poet and sportsman, wrote a number of plays in the 1950s and 1960s dealing with global political themes. In 1972 he opened a Centre for Creativity in Grenoble, developing training programmes that combine physical and dramatic skills.

17 École National Supérieure des Beaux-Arts teaches fine art and architecture and is one of the *grandes écoles* in which vocational

training is provided at the highest level to postgraduate students who have to pass a highly competitive entrance examination.

18 Lecoq says that the term 'mime' has become so reductive that we have to look for others. This is why he sometimes uses the term mimism (so well explained by Marcel Housse in his book *Anthropologie du geste*, published by Gallimard) which is not to be confused with mimicry. Mimicry is a representation of form, mimism is the search for the internal dynamics of meaning.

19 (*Hotel du libre échange*), *Heart's Desire Hotel* a farce by Georges Feydeau, published in a translation by Kenneth McLeish, Methuen, 2002, is a classic example of the 'French farces' of marital infidelity which were a feature of the late nineteenth-century French theatre.

20 Jean Gabin was a film actor noted for performing roles portraying the common man caught up in events beyond his control. He performed in films by Jean Renoir, Marcel Carné and other celebrated directors of the 1930s, 40s and 50s.

21 The Living Theatre is an avant-garde theatre company formed in New York in the 1950s by Julian Beck and Judith Malina. The company was invited to perform *Paradise Now* at the 1968 Avignon Theatre Festival, and took the opportunity to question the whole international theatre circuit, claiming that it had the right to perform its work free to all-comers, and helping to stir up the revolutionary atmosphere in France at the time. Methuen's book *The Living Theatre* by John Tytell was published in 1995.

22 In the late seventeenth and eighteenth centuries the Comédie Française exercised a monopoly on the use of spoken drama. This was abolished under the Revolution, only to be re-established by Napoleon, before being gradually eroded in the course of the nineteenth century.

23 Deburau was a famous nineteenth-century mime artist brought to life by Marcel Carné in his film *Les Enfants du Paradis*, with Jean-Louis Barrault giving one of his finest performances in the role of Deburau.

24 Steven Berkoff's collected plays are published by Faber.

25 Honoré Daumier was a celebrated artist, caricaturist and painter of nineteenth-century French society. He is especially remembered for his satirical portraits of social types, in which a predominantly realist pictorial style is pushed towards the grotesque.

26 Angela Davis was a leader of the Civil Rights movement in the United States of America.

27 André Malraux was a novelist, art historian and minister of culture

under de Gaulle, 1958–69.

28 Jean Moulin was a heroic resistance leader who was captured, tortured and killed under the Nazis in 1943. His remains were re-interred at the Panthéon in 1964.

29 Charles de Gaulle was leader of the Free French Forces resisting the German Occupation of France in the Second World War, and became the interim President of the new Republic after the liberation in 1944. He soon retired from political life, however, and it was not until 1958 that he was re-elected President as the only man considered capable of resolving the crisis of the colonial war in Algeria. In 1967, at a time when the movement for the liberation of Quebec was growing, he made a state visit to Canada during which he concluded one of his official orations with the inflamatory words 'Vive le Québec libre/Long live free Quebec'.

30 Jean Vilar, see note 15.

31 Roberto Rossellini was the most noted film director of the Italian neo-realist school, which emerged in the immediate aftermath of the Second World War. His work was much praised by André Bazin, first editor of *Les Cahiers du Cinéma*, and was influential in the emergence of the French New Wave directors of the 1960s, such as Jean-Luc Godard and François Truffaut.

32 Botho Strauss was a German playwright who came to prominence in the 1980s and 1990s with plays presenting the anguish of modern urban life in bleak, fragmentary scenes.

33 Michel Azama is a French playwright who trained at the Lecoq school. His play *Croisades* appeared in an English translation by Nigel Gearing as *Crossfire* (Oberon Books, 1993).

34 Antoine Vitez was a director, actor, translator, teacher, and the only person to have taught at Lecoq's school without having first been trained there. Vitez was known for challenging productions, often adaptations of Russian classics, which allowed great freedom to his actors. He directed the Théâtre de Chaillot throughout the 1980s, was appointed general administrator of the Comédie Française in 1988, but died only two years later in 1990.

35 Ariane Mnouchkine is probably the most celebrated theatre director in France today. She trained with Lecoq in the 1960s when her company, the Théâtre du Soleil, was in its infancy and went on to create a series of vigorous, imaginative *créations collectives* (collectively devised productions). In the 1980s and 1990s, she worked closely with Hélène

Cixous, who wrote several plays for her company. Her work is noted for its colourful, physically expressive style.

36 Saint-John Perse was a French poet (real name Alexis Saint-Léger) who spent much of his working life as a diplomat, published lyric poetry on the themes of childhood and exile, and was awarded the Nobel Prize in 1960.

AFTERWORD TO THE 2002 EDITION

Since the death of its founder, the Lecoq school has continued to flourish, perpetuating and developing the techniques and skills on which his teaching was based. We have started to save the 400 hours of film documenting Lecoq's teaching in digital form, which will soon be made available for educational use, and have established a staff of teachers who were all originally taught by Jacques. I work in close partnership with them while following the basic two-year structure that he originally established.

A new addition to the school's activities is the *atelier d'ecriture* [writing workshop] run by the playwright Michel Azama (who is also a graduate of the school). In this, he explores the implications of Lecoq's own reflections on language and the shape and sonority of individual words. Just as Lecoq taught his students to observe the world around them, so Azama's writing workshop states as its first objective: 'To learn to work with materials situated outside oneself: posters, photos, objects, emblems, dictionaries, places, fragments of text, quotations, mythologies, etc.'

There are other new developments, such as an experimental voice class for second-year students. Pascale Lecoq and Krikor Belekian now run the L.E.M., which grew from the work of the school and whose focus is chiefly on stage design. Given Lecoq's fundamental insight that everything moves [*tout bouge*], it is inconceivable that change should not be welcomed and embraced by those responsible for passing on his vision. The school has a steady flow of new students and will continue to find new forms of creation and experimentation for many years to come.

Fay Lecoq
Paris, December 2001

Tout bouge.
Tout évolue, progresse.
Tout se ricochette et se réverbère.
D'un point à un autre, pas de ligne droite.
D'un port à un port, un voyage.
Tout bouge, moi aussi!
Le bonheur et le malheur, mais le heurt aussi.
Un point indécis, flou, confus, se dessine,
Point de convergences,
Tentation d'un point fixe,
Dans un calme de toutes les passions.
Point d'appui et point d'arrivée,
Dans ce qui n'a ni commencement ni fin.
Le nommer,
Le rendre vivant,
Lui donner autorité
Pour mieux comprendre ce qui bouge,
Pour mieux comprendre le Mouvement.

Everything moves.
Everything develops and progresses.
Everything rebounds and resonates.
From one point to another, the line is never straight.
From harbour to harbour, a journey.
Everything moves ... as do I!
Joy and sorrow, confrontation too.
A vague point appears, hazy and confused,
A point of convergence,
The temptation of a fixed point,
In the calm of all the passions.
Point of departure and point of destination,
In what has neither beginning nor end.
Naming it,
Endowing it with life,
Giving it authority
For a better understanding of what moves
A better understanding of what Movement is.

Jacques Lecoq
Belle Ile en Mer
August 1997

Methuen Drama would like to thank the following photographers for their contributions to the book:

Alain Chambaretaud
Dodi Disanto
Michèle Laurent
Patrick Lecoq
Richard Lecoq

The figurative images were all drawn by Jacques Lecoq.